CE

C000133236

Release, Control and Validation
ITIL® Intermediate Capability Handbook

*it*SMF International
The IT Service Management Forum

London: TSO

information & publishing solutions

Published by TSO (The Stationery Office)
and available from:

Online
www.tsoshop.co.uk

Mail, Telephone, Fax & E-mail
TSO
PO Box 29, Norwich, NR3 1GN
Telephone orders/General enquiries:
0870 600 5522
Fax orders: 0870 600 5533
E-mail: customer.services@tso.co.uk
Textphone: 0870 240 3701

TSO@Blackwell and other Accredited Agents

The AXELOS swirl logo is a trade mark of
AXELOS Limited

The AXELOS logo is a trade mark of
AXELOS Limited

ITIL® is a registered trade mark of
AXELOS Limited

MSP® is a registered trade mark of
AXELOS Limited

P3O® is a registered trade mark of
AXELOS Limited

PRINCE2® is a registered trade mark of
AXELOS Limited

M_o_R® is a registered trade mark of
AXELOS Limited

The Best Management Practice Portfolio
Product logo is a trade mark of AXELOS Limited

A CIP catalogue record for this book is available
from the British Library

A Library of Congress CIP catalogue record has
been applied for

First edition 2009
Second edition 2013
First published 2013
Second impression 2015

ISBN 9780113314331 Single copy ISBN
ISBN 9780113314348 (Sold in a pack of 10 copies)

Printed in the United Kingdom for The
Stationery Office

Material is FSC certified and produced using
ECF pulp, sourced from fully sustainable forests

P002600254   10/13

Contents

Acknowledgements   ix

About this guide   xi

1   Introduction to service management   1
     1.1   Best practice (ST 2.1.7)   1
     1.2   The ITIL framework (ST 1.2, 1.4)   2
     1.3   Service management   5
     1.4   Processes and functions (ST 2.2.2, 2.2.3)   7
     1.5   Roles   10
     1.6   Release, control and validation supporting the
            service lifecycle   14

2   Change management   23
     2.1   Purpose and objectives (ST 4.2.1)   23
     2.2   Scope (ST 4.2.2)   23
     2.3   Value to the business (ST 4.2.3)   24
     2.4   Policies, principles and basic concepts (ST 4.2.4)   25
     2.5   Process activities, methods and techniques
            (ST 4.2.5)   29
     2.6   Managing organization and stakeholder change
            (ST 5.2)   34
     2.7   Triggers, inputs, outputs and interfaces (ST 4.2.6)   36
     2.8   Critical success factors and key performance
            indicators (ST 4.2.8)   38
     2.9   Challenges and risks   39

2.10   Typical day-to-day activities performed by service
operation (SO 5.12.1, 8.1)   40

2.11   Roles and responsibilities (ST 6.4.6)   41

3   **Service asset and configuration management**   **44**

3.1   Purpose and objectives (ST 4.3.1)   44

3.2   Scope (ST 4.3.2)   44

3.3   Value to the business (ST 4.3.3)   45

3.4   Policies, principles and basic concepts (ST 4.3.4)   45

3.5   Process activities, methods and techniques
(ST 4.3.5)   49

3.6   Asset management (ST 4.3.4.4)   53

3.7   Triggers, inputs, outputs and interfaces (ST 4.3.6) 54

3.8   Information management (ST 4.3.7)   55

3.9   Critical success factors and key performance
indicators (ST 4.3.8)   55

3.10   Challenges and risks   56

3.11   Typical day-to-day activities performed by service
operation (SO 5.12.2)   58

3.12   Roles and responsibilities (ST 6.4.7)   58

4   **Service validation and testing**   **60**

4.1   Purpose and objectives (ST 4.5.1)   60

4.2   Scope (ST 4.5.2)   60

4.3   Value to the business (ST 4.5.3)   61

4.4   Policies, principles and basic concepts (ST 4.5.4)   62

4.5   Process activities, methods and techniques
(ST 4.5.5)   69

4.6   Triggers, inputs, outputs and interfaces (ST 4.5.6) 73

4.7   Information management (ST 4.5.7)   74

	4.8	Critical success factors and key performance indicators (ST 4.5.8)	75
	4.9	Challenges and risks	75
	4.10	Roles and responsibilities (ST 6.4.9)	76
5	**Release and deployment management**		**78**
	5.1	Purpose and objectives (ST 4.4.1)	78
	5.2	Scope (ST 4.4.2)	78
	5.3	Value to the business (ST 4.4.3)	78
	5.4	Policies, principles and basic concepts (ST 4.4.4)	79
	5.5	Process activities, methods and techniques (ST 4.4.5)	81
	5.6	Triggers, inputs, outputs and interfaces (ST 4.4.6)	91
	5.7	Information management (ST 4.4.7)	92
	5.8	Critical success factors and key performance indicators (ST 4.4.8)	93
	5.9	Challenges and risks (ST 4.4.9)	93
	5.10	Typical day-to-day activities performed by service operation (SO 5.12.3)	94
	5.11	Roles and responsibilities (ST 6.4.8)	94
6	**Request fulfilment**		**97**
	6.1	Purpose and objectives (SO 4.3.1)	97
	6.2	Scope (SO 4.3.2)	97
	6.3	Value to the business and service lifecycle (SO 4.3.3)	98
	6.4	Policies, principles and basic concepts (SO 4.3.4)	98
	6.5	Process activities, methods and techniques (SO 4.3.5)	100
	6.6	Triggers, inputs, outputs and interfaces (SO 4.3.6)	103

6.7	Information management (SO 4.3.7)	104
6.8	Critical success factors and key performance indicators (SO 4.3.8)	105
6.9	Challenges and risks (SO 4.3.9)	106
6.10	Roles and responsibilities (SO 6.7.7)	107

7	**Change evaluation**	**109**
7.1	Purpose and objectives (ST 4.6.1)	109
7.2	Scope (ST 4.6.2)	109
7.3	Value to the business (ST 4.6.3)	110
7.4	Policies, principles and basic concepts (ST 4.6.4)	110
7.5	Process activities, methods and techniques (ST 4.6.5)	111
7.6	Triggers, inputs, outputs and interfaces (ST 4.6.6)	117
7.7	Information management (ST 4.6.7)	118
7.8	Critical success factors and key performance indicators (ST 4.6.8)	118
7.9	Challenges and risks (ST 4.6.9)	119
7.10	Roles and responsibilities (ST 6.4.10)	120

8	**Knowledge management**	**121**
8.1	Purpose and objectives (ST 4.7.1)	121
8.2	Scope (ST 4.7.2)	122
8.3	Value to the business (ST 4.7.3)	122
8.4	Policies, principles and basic concepts (ST 4.7.4)	123
8.5	Process activities, methods and techniques (ST 4.7.5)	126
8.6	Triggers, inputs, outputs and interfaces (ST 4.7.6)	128
8.7	Information management (ST 4.7.7)	129

	8.8	Critical success factors and key performance indicators (ST 4.7.8)	129
	8.9	Challenges and risks (ST 4.7.9)	130
	8.10	Relationship with continual service improvement (CSI 3.7)	131
	8.11	Roles and responsibilities (ST 6.4.11)	131
9	**Technology and implementation**		**133**
	9.1	Generic requirements for IT service management technology (SO 7.1)	133
	9.2	Evaluation criteria for technology and tools (SD 7.2)	134
	9.3	Practices for process implementation	135
	9.4	Challenges, critical success factors and risks relating to implementing practices and processes	138
	9.5	Planning and implementing service management technologies (SO 8.5)	140
	9.6	Technology for implementing collaboration, configuration management and knowledge management	142
	9.7	The Deming Cycle (CSI 3.7, 3.8, 5.5)	145
10	**Qualifications**		**147**
	10.1	Overview	147
	10.2	Foundation level	147
	10.3	Intermediate level	147
	10.4	ITIL Expert	149
	10.5	ITIL Master	149

11	**Related guidance (ST Appendix C)**	**150**
11.1	ITIL guidance and web services	150
11.2	Quality management system	150
11.3	Risk management	150
11.4	Governance of IT	151
11.5	COBIT	151
11.6	ISO/IEC 20000 service management series	151
11.7	Environmental management and green and sustainable IT	152
11.8	ISO standards and publications for IT	153
11.9	ITIL and the OSI framework	153
11.10	Programme and project management	153
11.11	Organizational change	154
11.12	Skills Framework for the Information Age	154
11.13	Carnegie Mellon: CMMI and eSCM frameworks	155
11.14	Balanced scorecard	155
11.15	Six Sigma	156

Further guidance and contact points	**157**
Glossary	**160**

Acknowledgements

SECOND EDITION

Author
Duncan Anderson, Global Knowledge

Reviewers
Oghale Efue, Epsom & Ewell Borough Council
Trevor Murray, The Grey Matters, UK
Paul Wigzel, Paul Wigzel Training & Consultancy

Series editor
Alison Cartlidge, Steria

FIRST EDITION

Authors
Tricia Lewin, independent consultant, UK
Stuart Rance, HP
Paul Wigzel, Paul Wigzel Training & Consultancy

Reviewers
John Groom, West Groom Consulting, UK
Ashley Hanna, HP, UK

Dave Jones, Pink Elephant, UK

Michael Imhoff Nielsen, IBM, Denmark

Aidan Lawes, service management evangelist, UK

Trevor Murray, The Grey Matters, UK

Michael Nyhuis, Solisma, Australia

Sue Shaw, Tricentrica, UK

HP Suen, The Hong Kong Jockey Club

Editors

Mark Lillycrop, *it*SMF UK

Stuart Rance, HP

About this guide

This guide provides a quick reference to the processes covered by the ITIL® release, control and validation (RCV) syllabus. It is designed to act as a study aid for students taking the ITIL Capability qualification for RCV, and as a handy portable reference source for practitioners who work with these processes.

This guide is not intended to replace the more detailed ITIL publications (Cabinet Office, 2011), nor to be a substitute for a course provider's training materials. Many parts of the syllabus require candidates to achieve competence at Bloom Levels 3 and 4, showing the ability to apply their learning and analyse a situation. This study aid focuses on the core knowledge that candidates need to acquire at Bloom Levels 1 and 2, including a knowledge and comprehension of the material that supports the syllabus.

Further syllabus details can be found at:

www.itil-officialsite.com/Qualifications/ITILQualificationScheme.aspx

Listed below in alphabetical order are the ITIL service management processes with cross-references to the publication in which they are primarily defined, and where significant further expansion is provided. Most processes play a role during each lifecycle stage, but only significant references are included. Those processes and functions specifically relevant to the RCV syllabus and covered in this guide are also listed.

ITIL service management processes

Service management process	RCV syllabus	Primary source	Further expansion
Access management		SO	
Availability management		SD	CSI
Business relationship management		SS	SD, CSI
Capacity management		SD	SO, CSI
Change evaluation	✔	ST	
Change management	✔	ST	
Demand management		SS	SD
Design coordination		SD	
Event management		SO	
Financial management for IT services		SS	
Incident management		SO	CSI
Information security management		SD	SO
IT service continuity management		SD	
Knowledge management	✔	ST	CSI
Problem management		SO	
Release and deployment management	✔	ST	

Service management process	RCV syllabus	Primary source	Further expansion
Request fulfilment	✔	SO	
Service asset and configuration management	✔	ST	
Service catalogue management		SD	SS
Service level management		SD	SS, CSI
Service portfolio management		SS	SD
Service validation and testing	✔	ST	
Seven-step improvement process		CSI	
Strategy management for IT services		SS	
Supplier management		SD	
Transition planning and support		ST	
Function			
Application management		SO	
IT operations management		SO	
Service desk		SO	
Technical management		SO	
SS *ITIL Service Strategy*; SD *ITIL Service Design*; ST *ITIL Service Transition*; SO *ITIL Service Operation*; CSI *ITIL Continual Service Improvement*			

1 Introduction to service management

Note that cross-references in the headings are to section numbers in the ITIL core publications, where more detail can be found. The abbreviations used are: SS *ITIL Service Strategy*; SD *ITIL Service Design*; ST *ITIL Service Transition*; SO *ITIL Service Operation*; and CSI *ITIL Continual Service Improvement*. The core publications are listed in the 'Further guidance and contact points' section at the end.

1.1 BEST PRACTICE (ST 2.1.7)

Organizations operating in dynamic environments need to improve their performance and maintain competitive advantage. Adopting best practices in industry-wide use can help to improve capability.

There are several sources for best practice:

- **Public frameworks and standards** These have been validated across diverse environments; knowledge is widely distributed among professionals; there is publicly available training and certification; acquisition of knowledge through the labour market is easier, as is collaboration and coordination across organizations
- **Proprietary knowledge of organizations and individuals** This is customized for the local context and specific business needs. It may only be available under commercial terms; it may also be tacit knowledge (i.e. inextricable and poorly documented).

1.2   THE ITIL FRAMEWORK (ST 1.2, 1.4)

The ITIL framework is a source of best practice in service management. It is:

- Vendor-neutral
- Non-prescriptive
- Best practice.

ITIL is successful because it describes practices that enable organizations to deliver benefits, return on investment and sustained success. This means that organizations can:

- Deliver value for customers through services, improving customer relationships
- Integrate the strategy for services with the business strategy and customer needs
- Measure, monitor and optimize IT services and service provider performance, and reduce costs
- Manage the IT investment and budget, risks, knowledge, capabilities and resources to deliver services effectively and efficiently
- Enable adoption of a standard approach to service management across the enterprise
- Change the organizational culture to support the achievement of sustained success.

ITIL guidance can be found in the following sets of publications:

- **ITIL core** Best-practice publications applicable to all types of organizations that provide services to a business
- **ITIL complementary guidance** A set of publications with guidance specific to industry sectors, organization types, operating models and technology architectures.

ITIL guidance can be adapted to support various business environments and organizational strategies. Complementary ITIL publications provide flexibility to implement the core in a diverse range of environments.

ITIL has been deployed successfully around the world for more than 20 years. Over this time, the framework has evolved from a specialized set of service management topics with a focus on function, to a process-based framework, which now provides a broader holistic service lifecycle.

> **Definition: service lifecycle**
>
> An approach to IT service management that emphasizes the importance of coordination and control across the various functions, processes and systems necessary to manage the full lifecycle of IT services. The service lifecycle approach considers the strategy, design, transition, operation and continual improvement of IT services. Also known as service management lifecycle.

The service lifecycle is described in the five ITIL core publications. Each of these covers a stage of the service lifecycle (see Figure 1.1), from the initial definition and analysis of business requirements in *ITIL Service Strategy* and *ITIL Service Design*, through migration into the live environment within *ITIL Service Transition*, to live operation and improvement in *ITIL Service Operation* and *ITIL Continual Service Improvement*.

Figure 1.1 The service lifecycle

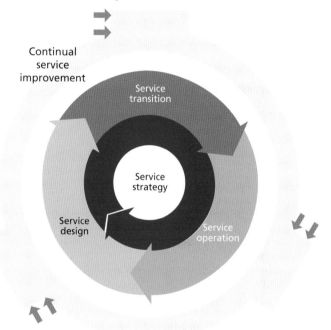

1.3   SERVICE MANAGEMENT

To understand what service management is, we need to understand what services are, and how service management can help service providers to deliver and manage these services.

Definition: service

A means of delivering value to customers by facilitating outcomes customers want to achieve without the ownership of specific costs and risks. The term 'service' is sometimes used as a synonym for core service, IT service or service package.

Definition: IT service

A service provided by an IT service provider. An IT service is made up of a combination of information technology, people and processes. A customer-facing IT service directly supports the business processes of one or more customers and its service level targets should be defined in a service level agreement (SLA). Other IT services, called supporting services, are not directly used by the business but are required by the service provider to deliver customer-facing services.

The outcomes that customers want to achieve are the reason why they purchase or use a service. The value of the service to the customer is directly dependent on how well a service facilitates these outcomes.

Definition: outcome

The result of carrying out an activity, following a process, or delivering an IT service etc. The term is used to refer to intended results as well as to actual results.

Services facilitate outcomes by enhancing the performance of associated tasks and reducing the effect of constraints. These constraints may include regulation, lack of funding or capacity, or technology limitations. The end result is an increase in the probability of desired outcomes. While some services enhance performance of tasks, others have a more direct impact – performing the task itself. Services can be classified as:

- **Core services** These deliver the basic outcomes desired by one or more customers
- **Enabling services** These are needed in order for a core service to be delivered
- **Enhancing services** These are added to core services to make them more appealing to the customer.

Service management enables service providers to:

- Understand the services they are providing
- Ensure that the services really do facilitate the outcomes their customers want to achieve
- Understand the value of the services to their customers
- Understand and manage all of the costs and risks associated with those services.

Definition: service management

A set of specialized organizational capabilities for providing value to customers in the form of services.

These 'specialized organizational capabilities' are described in this guide. They include the processes, activities, functions and roles that service providers use to enable them to deliver services to their customers, as well as the ability to organize, manage knowledge, and understand how to facilitate outcomes that create value. However, service management is more than just a set of capabilities. It is also a professional practice supported by an extensive body of knowledge, experience and skills, with formal schemes for the education, training and certification of practising organizations.

Service management is concerned with more than just delivering services. Each service, process or infrastructure component has a lifecycle, and service management considers the entire lifecycle from strategy through design and transition to operation and continual improvement.

All IT organizations should act as service providers, using the principles of service management to ensure that they deliver the outcomes required by their customers.

Definition: IT service management (ITSM)

The implementation and management of quality IT services that meet the needs of the business. IT service management is performed by IT service providers through an appropriate mix of people, process and information technology.

1.4   PROCESSES AND FUNCTIONS (ST 2.2.2, 2.2.3)

Definition: process

A process is a structured set of activities designed to accomplish a specific objective. A process takes one or more defined inputs and turns them into defined outputs. It may include any of the roles, responsibilities, tools and management controls required to reliably deliver the outputs. A process may define policies, standards, guidelines, activities and work instructions if they are needed.

Processes define actions, dependencies and sequence. Processes have the following characteristics:

- **Measurability** Processes can be measured and performance-driven, in management terms such as cost and quality, and in practitioner terms such as duration and productivity
- **Specific results** Processes exist to deliver a specific result that is identifiable and countable
- **Customers** Processes deliver their primary results to customers or stakeholders, either internal or external, to meet their expectations
- **Responsiveness to specific triggers** Processes may be ongoing or iterative, but should be traceable to a specific trigger.

The key outputs from any process are driven by the objectives and include process measurement, reports and improvement. For the process to be effective, process outputs have to conform to operational norms derived from business objectives. For the process to be efficient, process activities have to be undertaken with the minimum resources. Figure 1.2 illustrates a process model.

An organization needs to clearly define the roles and responsibilities required to undertake the processes and activities involved in each lifecycle stage. These roles are assigned to individuals within an organizational structure of teams, groups or functions.

Definition: function

A team or group of people and the tools or other resources they use to carry out one or more processes or activities – for example, the service desk.

Figure 1.2 Process model

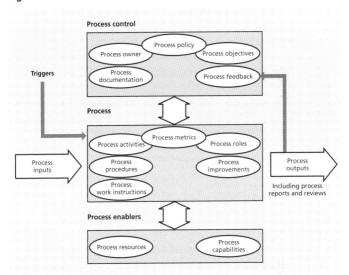

Functions are self-contained, and have the capabilities and resources necessary for their performance and outcomes. They provide organizations with structure and stability. Coordination between functions through shared processes is a common organizational design.

ITIL Service Operation describes the service desk, technical management, IT operations management and application management functions in detail, with technical and application management providing the technical resources and expertise to manage the whole service lifecycle.

1.5   ROLES

A role is a set of responsibilities, activities and authorities granted to a person or team. A role is defined in a process or function. One person or team may have multiple roles. ITIL does not describe all the roles that could possibly exist in an organization, but provides representative examples to aid in an organization's definition of its own roles.

Roles fall into two main categories – generic roles (e.g. process owner) and specific roles that are involved within a particular lifecycle stage or process. Generic roles are described below, while specific roles are covered in the relevant lifecycle chapters of the core ITIL publications.

Note that 'service manager' is a generic term for any manager within the service provider. The term is commonly used to refer to a business relationship manager, a process manager or a senior manager with responsibility for IT services overall. A service manager is often assigned several roles such as business relationship management, service level management and continual service improvement.

1.5.1   Process owner (ST 6.4.2)

The process owner role is accountable for ensuring that a process is fit for purpose, i.e. that it is capable of meeting its objectives; that it is performed according to the agreed and documented standard; and that it meets the aims of the process definition. This role may be assigned to the same person carrying out the process manager role.

Key accountabilities include:

- Sponsoring, designing and change managing the process and its metrics

- Defining the process strategy, with periodic reviews to keep current, and assisting with process design
- Defining appropriate policies and standards for the process, with periodic auditing to ensure compliance
- Communicating process information or changes as appropriate to ensure awareness
- Providing process resources to support activities required throughout the service lifecycle
- Ensuring that process technicians understand their role and have the required knowledge to deliver the process
- Addressing issues with the running of the process
- Identifying enhancement and improvement opportunities and making improvements to the process.

1.5.2 Process manager (ST 6.4.3)

The process manager role is accountable for operational management of a process. There may, for example, be several process managers for one process in different locations. This role may be assigned to the same person carrying out the process owner role.

Key accountabilities include:

- Working with the process owner to plan and coordinate all process activities
- Ensuring that all activities are carried out as required throughout the service lifecycle
- Appointing people to the required roles and managing assigned resources
- Working with service owners and other process managers to ensure the smooth running of services
- Monitoring and reporting on process performance

- Identifying opportunities for and making improvements to the process.

1.5.3 Process practitioner (ST 6.4.4)

A process practitioner is responsible for carrying out one or more process activities. This role may be assigned to the same person carrying out the process manager role.

Responsibilities typically include:

- Carrying out one or more activities of a process
- Understanding how his or her role contributes to the overall delivery of service and creation of value for the business
- Working with other stakeholders, such as line managers, co-workers, users and customers, to ensure that their contributions are effective
- Ensuring that the inputs, outputs and interfaces for his or her activities are correct
- Creating or updating records to show that activities have been carried out correctly.

1.5.4 Service owner (ST 6.4.1)

The service owner is responsible to the customer for the initiation, transition and ongoing maintenance and support of a particular service and is accountable to the IT director or service management director for the delivery of a specific IT service. The service owner's accountability for a specific service within an organization is independent of where the underpinning technology components, processes or professional capabilities reside.

Service ownership is critical to service management and one person may fulfil the service owner role for more than one service. Key responsibilities include:

- Ensuring that the ongoing service delivery and support meet agreed customer requirements via effective service monitoring and performance
- Working with business relationship management to ensure that the service provider can meet customer requirements
- Ensuring consistent and appropriate communication with customers for service-related enquiries and issues
- Representing the service across the organization; for example, by attending change advisory board (CAB) meetings
- Serving as the point of escalation (notification) for major incidents relating to the service
- Participating in internal and external service review meetings
- Participating in negotiating SLAs and operational level agreements (OLAs) relating to the service
- Identifying opportunities for, and making, improvements to the service.

The service owner is responsible for continual improvement and the management of change affecting the service under their care. The service owner is a primary stakeholder in all of the underlying IT processes which enable or support the service they own.

1.5.5 The RACI model (ST 6.5)

Roles are accountable to, or responsible for, an activity. However, as services, processes and their component activities run through an entire organization, each activity must be clearly mapped to well-defined roles. To support this, the RACI model or 'authority matrix' can be used to define the roles and responsibilities in relation to processes and activities.

RACI is an acronym for:

- **Responsible** The person or people responsible for correct execution (i.e. for getting the job done)
- **Accountable** The person who has ownership of quality and the end result. Only one person can be accountable for each task
- **Consulted** The people who are consulted and whose opinions are sought. They have involvement through input of knowledge and information
- **Informed** The people who are kept up to date on progress. They receive information about process execution and quality.

Only one person should be accountable for any process or individual activity, although several people may be responsible for executing parts of the activity.

1.6   RELEASE, CONTROL AND VALIDATION SUPPORTING THE SERVICE LIFECYCLE

Release, control and validation form the core of the service transition stage of the service lifecycle. The key principles of this stage are outlined here.

1.6.1   Purpose and objectives (ST 1.1.1)

The purpose of the service transition stage of the service lifecycle is to ensure that new, modified or retired services meet the expectations of the business as documented in the service strategy and service design stages of the lifecycle.

The objectives of service transition are to:

- Plan and manage service changes efficiently and effectively
- Manage risks relating to new, changed or retired services
- Successfully deploy service releases into supported environments
- Set correct expectations on the performance and use of new or changed services
- Ensure that service changes create the expected business value
- Provide good-quality knowledge and information about services and service assets.

1.6.2 Scope (ST 1.1.2)

The scope of service transition includes planning, building, testing, evaluation and deployment of all changes to services and service assets. Consideration is given to:

- Managing the complexity associated with changes to services and processes
- Allowing for innovation while minimizing the unintended consequences of change
- Introducing new services
- Changing existing services (e.g. expanding, reducing or changing suppliers)
- Retiring services, applications or other configuration items (CIs).

The scope of service transition includes guidance on transferring services:

- Out to a new supplier (outsourcing or offshoring), in from a supplier (insourcing), or out to a shared service provision
- From one supplier to another
- To multiple suppliers (smart sourcing), partnering or joint ventures

■ As part of mergers and acquisitions.

The scope also includes the transition of changes in a service provider's service management capabilities that will impact on the ways of working, the organization, people, projects and third parties involved in service management.

1.6.3 Value to business of service transition activities (ST 1.1.4)

Adopting and implementing standard and consistent approaches for service transition will:

■ Enable projects to plan the service transition stage more accurately, allowing service transition assets to be shared and re-used
■ Result in higher volumes of successful change
■ Improve expectation-setting for all stakeholders involved in service transition including customers, users, suppliers, partners and projects
■ Increase confidence that the new or changed service can be delivered to specification without unexpectedly affecting other services or stakeholders
■ Ensure that new or changed services will be maintainable and cost-effective.

1.6.4 Transition strategy (ST 4.1.5.1)

The organization should decide on the most appropriate approach to service transition based on the size and nature of the services, the number and frequency of releases required, and any special needs of the users, such as the requirement for phased deployments over an extended period of time.

The service transition strategy defines the overall approach to organizing service transition and allocating resources, including:

- Purpose and objectives of service transition
- Context (e.g. service customer, contract agreement portfolio)
- Scope (inclusions and exclusions)
- Applicable standards, agreements, legal, regulatory and contractual requirements
- Organizations and stakeholders involved in transition
- Framework for service transition, including criteria, approach and deliverables
- Identification of requirements and content of the new or changed service
- Schedule of milestones
- Financial requirements (budgets and funding).

1.6.5 Service transition lifecycle stages (ST 4.1.5.2)

The service design package (SDP) defines the lifecycle stages for service transition. The move from one stage to the next is subject to formal checks. Typical stages in the life of a transition include:

- Acquire and test new CIs and components
- Build and test
- Service release test
- Service operational readiness test
- Deployment
- Early life support
- Review and close service transition.

Each stage has exit and entry criteria and a list of mandatory deliverables.

1.6.6   Preparing for service transition (ST 4.1.5.3)

The service transition preparation activities include:

- Reviewing and acceptance of inputs from the other service lifecycle stages
- Reviewing and checking the input deliverables, such as the change proposal, SDP, service acceptance criteria and evaluation report
- Identifying, raising and scheduling requests for change (RFCs)
- Checking that the configuration baselines are recorded in the configuration management system (CMS) before the start of service transition
- Checking transition readiness.

Configuration baselines fix a point in history to which people can refer and apply changes.

Any variance in the proposed service scope, service strategy requirements and service design baseline must be requested and managed through change management.

1.6.7   Planning and coordinating service transition (ST 4.1.5.4)

1.6.7.1   Planning an individual service transition

The release and deployment management activities should be planned in stages as deployment requirements may not be known in detail initially. Each service transition plan should be developed from a proven service transition model.

A service transition plan describes the tasks and activities required to release and deploy a release into the test environments and into production, including:

- Work environment and infrastructure for the service transition
- Schedule of milestones, handover and delivery dates
- Activities and tasks to be performed
- Staffing, resource requirements, budgets and timescales at each stage
- Issues and risks to be managed
- Lead times and contingency.

1.6.7.2 Integrated planning

Good planning and management are essential for successful deployment of a release into production across distributed environments and locations. You should maintain an integrated set of transition plans that are linked to lower-level plans such as release build and test plans. Integrate these plans with the change schedule and release and deployment management plans.

Good-quality plans enable service transition to manage and coordinate the service transition resources (e.g. resource allocation, utilization, budgeting and accounting).

1.6.7.3 Adopting programme and project management best practice

It is best practice to manage several releases and deployments as a programme, with each significant deployment run as a project. This is typically based on PRINCE2 or PMBOK. The actual deployment may be carried out either by dedicated staff as part of broader responsibilities, such as operations, or through a team brought together for the purpose. Elements of the deployment may be delivered through external suppliers.

1.6.7.4   Reviewing the plans

Review all service transition and release and deployment plans. Lead times should include an element of contingency and be based on experience rather than just the supplier's assertion; this includes internal suppliers where there is no formal contract. Lead times typically vary depending on season, and this should be factored into planning. This is particularly true for long transitions, where the lead times may also vary between stages of a transition, or between different user locations.

1.6.8   Provide service transition support (ST 4.1.5.5)

1.6.8.1   Advice

Service transition provides support for all stakeholders to enable them to understand and follow the service transition framework of processes, supporting systems and tools. Although the transition planning and support team may not have the specialist resources to handle some issues, it needs to be able to identify relevant resources that can help projects.

1.6.8.2   Administration

Transition planning and support provides administration for:

- Managing service transition changes and work orders
- Managing issues, risks, deviations and waivers
- Managing support for tools and service transition processes
- Monitoring the service transition performance to provide input into continual service improvement.

Changes that affect the agreed baseline CIs are controlled through change management.

1.6.8.3 Communication

Managing communication throughout a service transition is critical to success. A communication plan should include:

- Objectives of the communication
- Defined stakeholders, including users, customers, IT staff, suppliers and customers of the business (if appropriate)
- Communication content for each type of stakeholder
- Communication frequency (daily, weekly etc.); this may vary for each stakeholder group at different stages of the transition
- Channel and format (newsletters, posters, emails, reports, presentations etc.)
- How the success of the communication will be measured.

1.6.8.4 Progress monitoring and reporting

Monitor service transition activities against the intentions set out in the transition model and plan. Measuring and monitoring the release and deployment establishes whether the transition is proceeding according to plan.

1.6.9 Processes within service transition

Service transition processes are:

- Transition planning and support
- Change management
- Service asset and configuration management
- Release and deployment management
- Service validation and testing
- Change evaluation
- Knowledge management.

The rest of this guide provides more information about the processes that are included in the release, control and validation curriculum. It is important to remember that these are only a small part of the entire service lifecycle described in this chapter, and they should be studied in the context of that lifecycle.

2 Change management

2.1 PURPOSE AND OBJECTIVES (ST 4.2.1)

Changes arise for a variety of reasons:

- **Proactively** Seeking business benefits such as growth, reduced costs, improved services, or increased effectiveness of support
- **Reactively** As a means of resolving errors and adapting to changing circumstances.

The purpose of the change management process is to control the lifecycle of all changes, enabling beneficial changes to be made with minimum disruption to IT services.

The objectives of change management are to:

- Respond to changing business requirements, while maximizing value and reducing incidents, disruption and rework
- Respond to requests for change (RFCs) from the business and IT that will align the services with the business needs
- Ensure changes are recorded and evaluated, and that authorized changes are prioritized, planned, tested, implemented, documented and reviewed in a controlled manner
- Ensure that all changes to CIs are recorded in the configuration management system (CMS)
- Optimize overall business risk.

2.2 SCOPE (ST 4.2.2)

The scope of change management includes changes to baselined service assets and CIs across the whole service lifecycle.

Each organization should define which changes are outside the scope of its service change process. Typically these include:

■ Changes with significantly wider impact than service changes, such as changes to business operations
■ Changes at an operational level, such as repair to a printer.

Figure 2.1 shows a typical scope for service change management for an IT department and how it interfaces with the business and suppliers at strategic, tactical and operational levels.

Figure 2.1 Scope of change management and release and deployment management for services

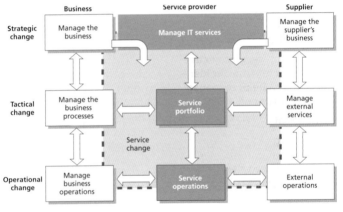

2.3   VALUE TO THE BUSINESS (ST 4.2.3)

Change management enables the service provider to add value to the business by:

- Protecting the business, and other services, while making required changes
- Implementing changes that meet customers' requirements while optimizing costs
- Contributing to governance, legal, contractual and regulatory requirements
- Reducing failed changes, service disruptions, defects and rework
- Improving service availability by improving the speed and success of corrective changes
- Reducing the time and effort needed to manage changes.

2.4 POLICIES, PRINCIPLES AND BASIC CONCEPTS (ST 4.2.4)

Change management needs executive support to implement a culture that sets stakeholder expectations about changes and releases. This helps to manage any pressures to reduce timescales, cut budgets or compromise testing.

Policies that support change management include:

- Creating a culture of change management across the organization where there is zero tolerance for unauthorized change
- Aligning with business, project and stakeholder change management
- Prioritization of change and management of change windows
- Establishing accountability, responsibilities and segregation of duties
- Preventing unauthorized change
- Performance and risk evaluation of all changes.

Change management should be planned with release and deployment management and service asset and configuration management. The design includes:

■ Requirements (legal, regulatory, standards, organizational practices)
■ Approach to eliminating unauthorized change
■ Techniques for identification and classification of changes
■ Roles and responsibilities (for authorization, testing, CAB membership, other stakeholders etc.)
■ Communication (changes, schedules, release plans)
■ Procedures for all change activities
■ Interfaces with other service management processes (especially configuration, release and deployment, incident and problem management).

2.4.1 Types of change request

A change request is a formal communication seeking an alteration to one or more CIs. This may be in the form of a request for change (RFC), but it could also be a service desk call, a formal request for change within a project, or some other similar formal communication.

Change management applies across the entire service lifecycle, not just during the operational stage. Table 2.1 provides examples of requests at different stages of the service lifecycle.

Table 2.1 Examples of requests by service lifecycle stage

Type of change	Documented work procedure	SS	SD	ST	SO	CSI
Change to service portfolio	Service change management	✔				
Change to service or service definition	Service change management	✔	✔	✔	✔	✔
Project change	Project change management procedure		✔	✔		✔
Operational activity	Local procedure (often pre-authorized)				✔	

There are three different types of service change:

■ **Standard change** A pre-authorized change that is low-risk, relatively common and follows a procedure or work instruction
■ **Emergency change** A change that must be implemented as soon as possible, for example to resolve a major incident or implement a security patch
■ **Normal change** Any service change that is not a standard change or an emergency change.

A change process model can help to ensure that a particular type of change is handled in a consistent way. The model may include:

- Steps to handle the change, including dependencies
- Roles and responsibilities
- Timescales and thresholds for completion of actions
- Escalation procedures.

Change proposals are submitted to change management before chartering new or changed services to ensure that potential conflicts for resources or other issues are identified. Authorization of the change proposal does not authorize implementation of the change but allows the service to be chartered so that service design activity can start.

A standard change is a change to a service or other CI for which the approach is pre-authorized by change management. This approach follows an accepted and established procedure to provide a specific change requirement. Every standard change has a change model that defines the steps to follow, including how the change is logged and managed as well as how it is implemented.

No change should be authorized unless you have explicitly defined what to do if it is not successful. A back-out plan enables the organization to be restored to its initial state, often through reloading a baselined set of CIs, especially software and data. If changes are not reversible an alternative approach to remediation is required, such as revisiting the change itself. If there are severe problems it may be necessary to invoke the organization's business continuity plan. By considering what remediation options are available before instigating a change and establishing that the remediation is viable, you can determine the risk of the proposed change and take the appropriate decisions.

2.5   PROCESS ACTIVITIES, METHODS AND TECHNIQUES (ST 4.2.5)

Figure 2.2 shows the process flow for a normal change.

Figure 2.2 Example of a process flow for a normal change

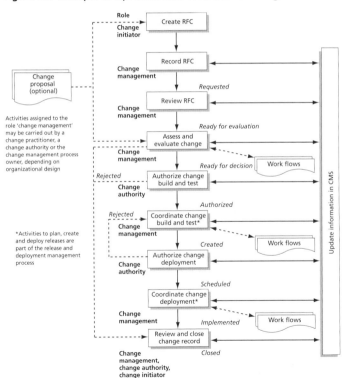

2.5.1   Create and record the request for change

The change initiator fills in an RFC, which ensures that all the required information is supplied. The RFC may be recorded on paper or electronically. Information in an RFC usually includes:

- Unique ID
- Description, including CIs and baselines to be changed
- Reason for the change, effects of not implementing it, and priority
- Category (minor, significant, major)
- Change authority for this change (usually based on category)
- Date and time, and details of the change initiator
- Predicted times and resources
- Implementation and back-out or remediation plans
- Impact and risk assessment, including effect on continuity plans.

If this is a major change with significant implications then a change proposal is required. A change proposal is used to communicate a high-level description of the change. This change proposal is normally created by the service portfolio management process and is passed to change management for authorization.

A change record is created, following a formal process. This record includes the information from the RFC, plus fields used to track the change during its lifecycle. Change records reference the CIs that are affected by the change and may be stored in the CMS or elsewhere in the service knowledge management system (SKMS).

2.5.2   Review request for change

Change management carries out an initial review and rejects changes that are incomplete, totally impractical, or that duplicate other RFCs (accepted, rejected or still under consideration).

Rejected RFCs are returned to the initiator with an explanation. The initiator has a right of appeal.

2.5.3   Assess and evaluate change

An assessment of the potential impact of the change is carried out. Many organizations have a specific impact assessment form for this. Generic questions such as the 'seven Rs' are a good starting point:

- Who **raised** the change?
- What is the **reason** for the change?
- What is the **return** required from the change?
- What are the **risks** involved in the change?
- What resources are **required** to deliver the change?
- Who is **responsible** for the build, test and implementation of the change?
- What is the **relationship** between this change and other changes?

Responsibility for carrying out the assessment must be defined. Final responsibility is with the service owner, who is represented on the CAB.

Considerations for an impact and resource assessment include:

- Impact on the customer's business operation
- Effect on the IT infrastructure and on non-IT infrastructure, such as security and transport
- Effect on the service and on other services
- Impact of not implementing the change
- IT, business and other resources needed to implement the change, and for ongoing support of the changed service
- The current change schedule and projected service outage

■ Impact on plans for continuity, capacity, security, testing and operation.

A risk assessment assigns a risk category, based on the probability and impact of the possible outcomes.

The change authority (see section 2.5.4) evaluates the change based on the impact and risk assessments. It also prioritizes the change based on impact and urgency. A typical change prioritization scheme is shown in Table 2.2. The change is then scheduled based on its priority, the existing change schedule and the release plans.

2.5.4 Authorize change

A change authority is responsible for the formal authorization of each change. This change authority may be a role, person or group of people and varies depending on the specific type of change.

The CAB includes suitable representation from all stakeholders. The members may meet electronically or face to face and review RFCs, successful and failed changes, schedules and the change management process itself.

Levels of authority for the various types of change are as follows:

■ For very significant changes the CAB may pass the request to a higher-level authority such as a global CAB, or the board of directors.
■ For minor changes the change authority may be an operations supervisor or the change manager, or another suitably placed person. This authority is defined as part of the overall change management process.
■ For emergency changes the change authority may be the emergency change advisory board (ECAB), if it is not practical to convene a meeting of the full CAB in the time available.

Table 2.2 Change priority examples

Priority	Corrective change	Enhancement change
Immediate (treat as emergency change)	Risk to life or the ability to continue in business	Not appropriate for enhancement requests
High	Severely affecting key users, or affecting many users	Meets legal requirements
		Response to short-term opportunity
Medium	No severe impact, but cannot be deferred until next release	Maintains business viability
		Supports planned initiatives
Low	Can wait until next release	Usability improvement
		Adds new facilities

2.5.5 Coordinate change implementation

Authorized change requests are formally passed to an appropriate technical group to build the change. This activity is carried out as part of the release and deployment management process.

Change management is responsible for coordinating activities to manage the change schedule. This includes ensuring all testing is complete, and that implementation and remediation plans are in place.

2.5.6 Review and close change record

The results of every change are reported for evaluation and presented as a completed change for stakeholder agreement. This evaluation is carried out as part of the evaluation process.

A change review or post-implementation review confirms the change has met its objectives. The review includes incidents caused by the change, and achievement of service targets by any third parties involved. Change management (or the CAB) decides what action to take if changes have not met their objectives.

2.6 MANAGING ORGANIZATION AND STAKEHOLDER CHANGE (ST 5.2)

Change is an inevitable and important part of organizational development and growth. Change can be incremental or sudden, affecting part or the whole of an organization, its people and its culture. Organizational change is an essential part of continual improvement and must be built into all transitions to enable them to deliver value to the business.

Organizational change efforts fail or fall short of their goals because changes and transitions are not led, managed and monitored efficiently across the organization and throughout the change process. These gaps in key organizational activities often result in employee resistance, dissatisfaction and increased costs.

The five key elements of change are necessity, vision, plan, resources and competence. It is important that management commits to these five requirements in any change.

The management board or executive must provide a clear strategic vision. It needs to ensure that there are adequate connections and controls throughout the organization to alert it to any barriers and to facilitate the transition to its goal.

Factors that drive successful organizational change initiatives include:

- Leadership for the change
- Organization adoption
- Governance
- Organization capabilities
- Business and service performance measures
- A strong communication process with regular opportunity for staff feedback.

While service transition is not accountable for the overall management of business and technical change, the service transition process owner or manager is a key stakeholder and needs to be proactive in reporting issues and risks to the change leaders.

Service transition must be actively involved in changing the mindsets of people across the lifecycle to ensure they are ready to play their role in service transition. These people include:

- Service transition staff
- Customers
- Users
- Service operation functions
- Suppliers
- Key stakeholders.

Service transition focuses on simple messages to ensure that there is consistency in the implementation of the changes. For example, service transition would be interested in helping people to:

- Understand the need for knowledge and effective knowledge transfer
- Understand the importance of making decisions at the right speed and within the appropriate timeframe
- Understand the need to complete and review configuration baselines in a timely manner
- Apply more effective risk assessment and management methods for service transition
- Follow the deadlines for submitting changes and releases.

2.7   TRIGGERS, INPUTS, OUTPUTS AND INTERFACES (ST 4.2.6)

RFCs may be triggered at any point in the service lifecycle, and by many different processes and organizations.

Strategic changes may arise from:

- Changes to legislation, regulations, policy or standards
- Organizational changes or changes to patterns of business activity
- Addition of new services or other updates to the service portfolio, customer portfolio or contract portfolio
- Sourcing changes and technology innovations.

Changes to planned services (in the service pipeline) and to existing services (in the service catalogue) may result in updates to:

- Service catalogue, service packages, definitions or characteristics

- Service level requirements, warranties or utilities
- Predicted capacity, quality, value or performance
- Release packages, acceptance criteria or communication plans
- Service assets (including infrastructure such as buildings)
- Processes or plans, such as capacity, IT service continuity management and test plans
- Procedures, measurement systems and documentation.

Some changes are a result of continual improvement activity; these also result in an RFC being submitted.

Operational changes, such as server reboots, may be done to correct or prevent incidents. These are often carried out as standard changes. Other operational changes may include requests to reset a password or move a service asset. These activities are often carried out as part of a request fulfilment process.

Inputs include:

- Policies, plans and strategies for change, release, deployment, evaluation etc.
- Change proposals and RFCs
- Change schedule and projected service outage
- Current assets, baselines, service packages, release packages etc.
- Test results, test reports and evaluation report.

Outputs include:

- Rejected and approved RFCs
- Updates to the service portfolio and service catalogue
- Changes to services and other CIs
- Revised change schedule and projected service outage
- Authorized change plans and updated change documentation, records and reports.

Interfaces within IT service management (ITSM) include:

- Service asset and configuration management (SACM)
- Problem management
- IT service continuity management
- Information security management
- Capacity management and demand management
- Service portfolio management.

Interfaces outside ITSM include:

- Business change processes
- Programme and project management
- Organizational and stakeholder change management
- Sourcing and partnering.

2.8   CRITICAL SUCCESS FACTORS AND KEY PERFORMANCE INDICATORS (ST 4.2.8)

The efficiency and effectiveness of the process can be measured by identifying critical success factors (CSFs) for the process, each CSF being supported by key performance indicators (KPIs):

- CSF Responding to RFCs from the business and IT that align the services with the business needs while maximizing value:
  - KPI Increase in the percentage of changes that meet the customer's agreed requirements; for example, quality, cost, time
  - KPI The benefits of change (expressed as 'value of improvements made' + 'negative impacts prevented or terminated') exceed the costs of change

- **CSF** Optimizing overall business risk:
  - KPI Reduction in the number of disruptions to services, defects and rework caused by inaccurate specification, poor or incomplete impact assessment
  - KPI Reduction in the percentage of changes that are categorized as emergency changes
- **CSF** Ensuring that all changes to CIs are well managed and recorded in the CMS:
  - KPI Reduction in the number and percentage of changes with incomplete change specifications
  - KPI Reduction in the number and percentage of changes with incomplete impact assessments.

2.9   CHALLENGES AND RISKS

Challenges include:

- Ensuring that every change is recorded and managed
- Being seen to facilitate change, rather than to introduce delays
- Implementing a true change management process that becomes involved early enough in the service lifecycle, includes assessment of benefits and costs, and helps to plan and manage changes
- Agreeing and documenting the many levels of change authority that are needed to manage change effectively and enabling effective communication between these change authorities.

Risks include:

- Lack of commitment to the change management process from the business, IT management or IT staff
- Implementation of changes without the use of change management

■ Change assessment being reduced to 'box-ticking', without real consideration of the risks, costs and benefits

■ Introducing delays to change implementation without adding sufficient value

■ Insufficient time or resources being allowed for proper assessment of changes, and pressure from projects or the business to expedite decisions

■ Insufficient time being allowed for implementation of changes, and attempting to fit too many changes into a change window

■ Lack of clarity on how change management interacts with other service management processes, project management or service design activities

■ Excessively bureaucratic change management processes that introduce excessive delay to required changes.

2.10   TYPICAL DAY-TO-DAY ACTIVITIES PERFORMED BY SERVICE OPERATION (SO 5.12.1, 8.1)

Change management is described in *ITIL Service Transition*, but many activities related to it are carried out during the service operation stage of the service lifecycle by people working in service operation functions:

■ Raising and submitting RFCs to address service operation issues

■ Assessing changes and participating in CAB or ECAB meetings

■ Implementing or backing out changes as directed by change management

■ Helping to define and maintain change models

■ Using the change management process for operational changes.

2.11   ROLES AND RESPONSIBILITIES (ST 6.4.6)

The roles of the CAB, emergency change advisory board (ECAB) and change authority are discussed in sections 2.5.3 and 2.5.4.

2.11.1 Change management process owner

Responsibilities include:

■ Carrying out the generic process owner role for the change management process (see section 1.5 for more detail)
■ Designing the change authority hierarchy and criteria for allocating RFCs to change authorities
■ Designing change models and workflows
■ Working with other process owners to ensure that there is an integrated approach to the design and implementation of change management, service asset and configuration management, release and deployment management, and service validation and testing.

2.11.2 Change management process manager

Responsibilities include:

■ Carrying out the generic process manager role for the change management process (see section 1.5 for more detail)
■ Receiving, logging and assigning priority to all RFCs and rejecting incomplete or totally impractical RFCs
■ Deciding whom to invite to CAB meetings, issuing invitations and agenda, and circulating RFCs in advance for review
■ Convening CAB or ECAB meetings, considering advice from the CAB or ECAB, and authorizing acceptable changes
■ Communicating with users and the business, including publishing the change schedule and projected service outage

- Coordinating the build, test and implementation of the change, and updating the change log with progress
- Reviewing all changes, identifying opportunities for improvement and producing management reports.

Depending on the size of the organization, the change management process manager may also be the process owner for the change management process.

2.11.3 Change initiator

Responsibilities include:

- Identifying the requirement for a change
- Completing and submitting a change proposal if appropriate
- Completing and submitting an RFC
- Attending CAB meetings to provide further information about the RFC or change proposal if invited
- Reviewing change when requested by change management, and specifically before closure.

Many different people in the organization may carry out this role; it is not usually carried out by people who work in change management. Each change has a single change initiator.

2.11.4 Change practitioner

Responsibilities include:

- Verifying that RFCs are correctly completed
- Allocating RFCs to appropriate change authorities based on defined criteria
- Submitting requests for evaluation to trigger the change evaluation process

- Formally communicating decisions of change authorities to affected parties
- Monitoring and reviewing activities of teams and functions that build and test changes to ensure that the work is carried out correctly
- Publishing the change schedule and projected service outage and ensuring that they are available when and where needed.

2.11.5 Change authority

Responsibilities include:

- Reviewing specific categories of RFC
- Formally authorizing changes at agreed points in the change lifecycle
- Participating in the change review before changes are closed
- Attending CAB meetings to discuss and review changes when required.

There are normally different change authorities for each category of change.

3 Service asset and configuration management

3.1 PURPOSE AND OBJECTIVES (ST 4.3.1)

No organization can be fully efficient or effective unless it manages its assets well, particularly those assets that are vital to the running of the customer's or organization's business. The purpose of the service asset and configuration management (SACM) process is to ensure that the assets required to deliver services are properly controlled, and that accurate and reliable information about those assets is available when and where it is needed. This information includes details of how the assets have been configured and the relationships between them.

The objective of SACM is to define and control components of services and infrastructure, and to maintain accurate information on the planned, current and historical state of services and infrastructure.

3.2 SCOPE (ST 4.3.2)

The scope of SACM depends on the size of the implementing organization, but some scoping statements are valid for implementations of any scale or with any objectives:

- Asset management covers the lifecycle of service assets from acquisition to disposal. It provides a complete inventory of assets and who is responsible for their control
- Configuration management ensures that components of a service, system or product are identified, baselined and maintained. It provides a configuration model of services,

assets and infrastructure by recording relationships between service assets and CIs
- SACM is accountable for the accuracy of the data within the configuration management system (CMS).

3.3 VALUE TO THE BUSINESS (ST 4.3.3)

SACM provides visibility of assets and CIs. The configuration model gives clear views of relationships and accurate representations of a service, release or environment. As such it provides business benefit by enabling:

- Changes and releases to be assessed, planned and delivered successfully
- Assistance in speeding up incident resolutions
- Better adherence to standards and regulatory obligations
- The ability to identify the full cost model of delivering a service
- Easy access to information on all assets and CIs held within the CMS
- Proper stewardship of fixed assets that are under the control of the service provider.

3.4 POLICIES, PRINCIPLES AND BASIC CONCEPTS (ST 4.3.4)

The first step is to develop and maintain the SACM policies that set the objectives, scope, principles and critical success factors (CSFs) for what is to be achieved by the process. These policies are often considered with the change management and release and deployment management policies because they are closely related. Asset policies may be applicable for specific asset types or services, such as desktop systems.

SACM needs change management to make it effective. The maintenance of the CMS is the responsibility of SACM, but change management enables the CMS's accuracy to be maintained.

Significant cost and resource commitments are required to implement SACM, so careful thought must be given to the scale and scope of implementation. Many IT service providers focus initially on the basic hardware and software assets, or on service assets that are business-critical or covered by legal and regulatory compliance.

Typical principles include:

- The need to meet corporate governance requirements such as Sarbanes-Oxley
- The need to deliver capability, resources and warranties defined by service level agreements (SLAs)
- The requirement for available, reliable and cost-effective services
- The application of whole-life cost appraisal methods
- The requirement to maintain asset and configuration information for stakeholders
- The level of control and requirements for traceability and auditability
- The provision of information for other business and service management processes.

3.4.1 The configuration model

SACM delivers a logical model of the services, assets and infrastructure by recording relationships between CIs. The real power of this model is that it is a single model, used by all parts of IT service management and beyond; it potentially includes human resources, finance, suppliers and customers. This enables other processes to access valuable information so they can:

- Assess the impact and cause of incidents and problems
- Assess the impact of proposed changes
- Plan and design new or changed services, technology refreshes and software upgrades
- Plan release and deployment packages, and migrate service assets to different locations and service centres.

3.4.2 Configuration items

CIs vary widely in complexity, size and type. A very complex CI might be an entire service or system, including hardware, software, documentation and support staff. This complex CI could be created from a large number of other, simpler CIs and components.

CIs are selected using established selection criteria, grouped, classified and identified in such a way that they are manageable and traceable throughout the service lifecycle.

Common categories for CIs include:

- **Service lifecycle CIs** Such as business cases, service management plans, service design packages (SDPs)
- **Service CIs** Including service capability assets (management, organization, processes, knowledge, people) and service resource assets (financial capital, systems, applications, information, data, infrastructure and facilities, people)
- **Organization CIs** Including functional hierarchies, social networks and organizational documentation
- **Internal CIs** Owned by the service provider
- **External CIs** Owned by customers, suppliers or subcontractors

- **Interface CIs** Required to deliver the end-to-end service across a service provider interface.

3.4.3 The configuration management system

To manage large and complex IT services and infrastructures, SACM requires the use of a CMS, with a layered architecture. This includes layers for data, information, knowledge processing and presentation.

The CMS holds all information for CIs within the designated scope. It maintains the relationships between CIs and related incidents, problems, known errors, change and release documentation. It may also include data about employees, suppliers, locations, customers and users.

The CMS includes one or more configuration management databases (CMDBs) and definitive media libraries (DMLs) as well as other data. It provides access to data in other inventories wherever possible, rather than duplicating data.

Automated processes to load CMDBs should be developed where possible, to reduce errors, maintain consistency and accuracy, and reduce costs.

The CMS integrates and manages a number of other SACM concepts, including:

- **Secure libraries** Collections of software, electronic or document CIs of known type and status, used to control and release components throughout the service lifecycle. Access to items in the library is restricted
- **DMLs** Secure libraries in which definitive authorized versions of all media CIs are stored and protected. The DML stores master copies of versions that have passed quality assurance checks. Only authorized media should be accepted into a DML, which is strictly controlled by SACM

- **Secure stores** Warehouses that store IT assets, such as those used for desktop deployment. A secure store maintains reliable access to equipment of known quality
- **Definitive spares** Components or assemblies in a secure store that are maintained at the same level as the comparative systems within the operational or controlled test environments
- **Baselines** A configuration baseline is the configuration of a service, product or infrastructure that has been formally reviewed and agreed upon. It serves as a basis for further activities and can be changed only through formal procedures. It captures the structure, contents and details of a configuration and represents a set of CIs that are related to each other
- **Snapshots** The state, at a particular time, of a CI or an environment, such as a discovery tool. Snapshots are recorded in the CMS and remain as fixed historical records.

3.5 PROCESS ACTIVITIES, METHODS AND TECHNIQUES (ST 4.3.5)

Figure 3.1 shows high-level activities for SACM. This model may be helpful where there are many parties, suppliers or activities that need to be established.

3.5.1 Management and planning

The management team decides on the scope and what level of detail is needed, and documents this in a configuration management plan. A typical plan includes:

- Scope
- Requirements
- Applicable policies and standards

- Organization for SACM
- System tools
- Application of processes and procedures
- Reference implementation plan
- Relationship management and control of suppliers and subcontractors.

There may also be separate configuration management plans for individual projects, services or groups of services.

Figure 3.1 Typical service asset and configuration management activity model

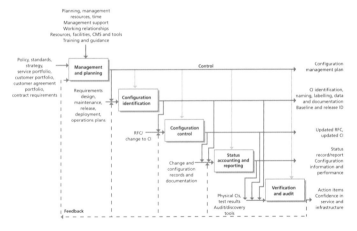

3.5.2 Configuration identification

When planning identification it is important to:

- **Define how CIs are to be selected, grouped, classified and defined** The important part of SACM is deciding the level at which control is to be exercised. Choosing the right CI level requires a balance between information availability, the right level of control and the effort needed. CI information is only valuable if it facilitates management of change, control of incidents and problems, or control of assets that can be independently moved, copied or changed. The organization should review the CI level regularly to check that information is still valuable and useful

- **Define the approach to identification, naming and labelling** Naming conventions are established and applied to identify CIs. Each CI has a unique identifier and version number. Physical CIs are labelled with the configuration identifier, and procedures are required to maintain the accuracy of labels

- **Define the roles and responsibilities of the CI owner** These are defined for each stage of the lifecycle.

Configuration identification steps are:

- Select the CIs based on documented criteria, and assign a unique name to each
- Specify the relevant attributes and relationships:
  - Attributes describe the characteristics of a CI that are valuable to record and that support service management processes

   – Relationships describe how the CIs work together; for
     example, a parent–child relationship; connected to; part
     of; or installed on. Relationships may be one-to-one,
     one-to-many or many-to-one; for example, many
     applications may be installed on one server
■ Specify when each CI is placed under configuration management;
   for example, when it is released and when it is acquired
■ Identify the owner of each CI.

3.5.3   Configuration control

Configuration control ensures that there are control mechanisms
over CIs, and maintains a record of changes to CIs, status, versions,
location and ownership. Without control of the physical or
electronic assets and components, configuration data and
information will not match the physical world.

No CI should be added, modified, replaced or removed without
an appropriate controlling procedure.

Control should be passed from a project or supplier to the service
provider at the scheduled time with accurate configuration
information, documentation and records.

3.5.4   Status accounting and reporting

Each asset or CI has one or more discrete states through which it
can progress. The list of valid status codes depends on the CI
type, as follows:

■ For a hardware component it might include: ordered,
   installed, in store, working, broken, approved, withdrawn
   and disposed of

■ For a service it might include: requirements, defined, analysed, approved, chartered, designed, developed, built, tested, released, operational and retired.

During configuration identification and control activities, configuration status records are created and modified. Status reporting provides current and historical data about each CI.

3.5.5   Verification and audit

These activities include a series of reviews or audits to:

■ Ensure there is conformity between the documented baselines and the actual business environment
■ Verify the physical existence of CIs and check that the records in the CMS match the physical infrastructure
■ Verify that every physical component has a record in the CMS
■ Check that required release and configuration documentation is in place before making a release.

Plans are needed to ensure regular configuration audits are carried out, to check that the CMDBs and related configuration information are consistent with the physical state.

3.6   ASSET MANAGEMENT (ST 4.3.4.4)

The fixed assets of an organization are assets that have a financial value, can be used by the organization to help create products or services and have a long-term useful life. For an IT service provider these may include data centres, power distribution and air-handling components, servers, software licences, network components, PCs, data or information. Most organizations have a process that manages these assets.

Software asset management is responsible for the management of software, software licences and codes for activating software – whether these are installed on computer systems or held as copies that could be installed. Software asset management includes management, control and protection of software assets and the risks arising from their use.

The IT service provider must implement appropriate and auditable procedures for software asset management. Ideally, these will be compliant with the international standard ISO/IEC 19770.

3.7   TRIGGERS, INPUTS, OUTPUTS AND INTERFACES (ST 4.3.6)

Updates to SACM information are triggered by changes, purchase orders, acquisitions and service requests.

Inputs include:

- Designs, plans and configurations from SDPs
- RFCs and work orders from change management
- Actual configuration information collected by tools and audits
- Information in the organization's fixed asset register.

Outputs include:

- New and updated configuration records
- Updated asset information for use in updating the fixed asset register
- Information about attributes and relationships of CIs, for use by all other service management processes
- Configuration snapshots and baselines
- Status reports and other consolidated configuration information
- Audit reports.

As the single repository for configuration data, SACM supports and interfaces with every other process, function and activity. There are strong relationships with:

- **Change management** Identifying impact of proposed changes
- **Financial management** Documenting financial information, such as cost and owner
- **IT service continuity management** Being aware of assets that the business service depends on, control of spares and software
- **Incidents, problems and errors** Maintaining diagnostic information and providing data for the service desk.

3.8   INFORMATION MANAGEMENT (ST 4.3.7)

Backup copies of the CMS are taken regularly and stored securely, preferably off-site to enable access when IT service continuity management is invoked.

The amount of historical information to be retained depends upon the usefulness of the data to the organization. The retention policy for historical records is reviewed regularly and amended if necessary.

3.9   CRITICAL SUCCESS FACTORS AND KEY PERFORMANCE INDICATORS (ST 4.3.8)

As with all processes, SACM is subject to regular monitoring and reporting, and action is taken when needed to implement continual improvement.

The efficiency and effectiveness of the process can be measured by identifying critical success factors (CSFs) for the process, each CSF being supported by key performance indicators (KPIs):

- **CSF** Accounting for, managing and protecting the integrity of CIs throughout the service lifecycle:
  - KPI Improved accuracy in budgets and charges for the assets utilized by each customer or business unit
  - KPI Increase in re-use and redistribution of under-utilized resources and assets
- **CSF** Supporting efficient and effective service management processes by providing accurate configuration information at the right time:
  - KPI Percentage improvement in maintenance scheduling over the life of an asset (not too much, not too late)
  - KPI Improved speed for incident management to identify faulty CIs and restore service
- **CSF** Establishing and maintaining an accurate and complete CMS:
  - KPI Reduction in business impact of outages and incidents caused by poor service asset and configuration management
  - KPI Increased quality and accuracy of configuration information.

3.10 CHALLENGES AND RISKS

Challenges include:

- Persuading technical support staff to adopt a policy of checking everything in and out – this can be perceived as a hindrance to a fast and responsive support service. If the positives of such a system are not conveyed adequately, staff may be inclined to try and circumvent it. Even then, resistance can still occur – placing this as an objective in annual appraisals is one way to help enforce the policy.

- Attracting and justifying funding for SACM, since it is typically unseen by the customer units empowered with funding control. In practice it is typically funded as an 'invisible' element of change management and other ITSM processes that are more visible to the business.
- An attitude of 'just collecting data because it is possible to do it'; this leads SACM into a data overload, which is impossible, or at least disproportionately expensive, to maintain.
- Lack of commitment and support from management who do not understand the key role SACM must play in supporting other processes.

Risks include:

- The temptation to consider SACM to be technically oriented rather than service and business focused, since technical competence is essential to its successful delivery
- Degradation of the accuracy of configuration information over time, which can cause errors and be difficult and costly to correct
- Setting the scope too wide, causing excessive cost and effort for insufficient benefit
- Setting the scope too narrow, so that the process has too little benefit
- The CMS becoming out of date due to the movement of hardware assets by non-authorized staff. To prevent this, undertake regular physical audits to highlight discrepancies, investigate them, and inform managers of any inconsistencies.

3.11 TYPICAL DAY-TO-DAY ACTIVITIES PERFORMED BY SERVICE OPERATION (SO 5.12.2)

There are a few activities carried out during the service operation stage of the lifecycle that directly contribute to the success of SACM:

- Informing SACM of any discrepancies found between CIs and the CMS
- Making agreed amendments to correct discrepancies.

Responsibility for updating the CMS remains with SACM, but in some cases staff working within service operation functions may be asked to update relationships, add new CIs or amend the status of CIs.

3.12 ROLES AND RESPONSIBILITIES (ST 6.4.7)

During the first stages of a project, the programme or project office may be responsible for configuration management. At defined release points this responsibility is passed to staff working within service transition, and SACM takes over the responsibility for CI documentation.

3.12.1 SACM process owner

Responsibilities include:

- Carrying out the generic process owner role for the SACM process (see section 1.5 for more detail)
- Agreeing the scope for SACM and policies
- Working with other process owners to ensure integration.

3.12.2 SACM process manager

Responsibilities include:

- Carrying out the generic process manager role for the SACM process (see section 1.5 for more detail)
- Responsible for planning, implementing, monitoring and improving configuration management as a process.

3.12.3 Configuration analyst

Responsibilities include:

- Working with the SACM process manager to plan aspects of configuration management, such as which CIs should be managed and to what level
- Training other configuration management staff and performing configuration audits.

3.12.4 Configuration librarian

Responsibilities include being the custodian and guardian of master copies of software, assets and documentation.

4 Service validation and testing

4.1 PURPOSE AND OBJECTIVES (ST 4.5.1)

The purpose of the service validation and testing process is to ensure that a new or changed IT service matches its design specification and meets the needs of the business.

The objectives of service validation and testing are to:

- Assure people that the new or changed services will provide the expected outcomes and value within the cost, capacity and constraints identified
- Validate a service to make sure that it is 'fit for purpose'
- Ensure that a service is 'fit for use'
- Confirm that requirements for new or changed services are defined correctly
- Find any errors and variances and remedy them early in the service lifecycle.

4.2 SCOPE (ST 4.5.2)

Service validation and testing can be applied throughout the service lifecycle to ensure the quality of:

- Any aspect of any new or changed service or service offering, including:
    - Services developed in-house or externally
    - Hardware, software or knowledge-based services
- The service provider's capability, resources and capacity to deliver a service or service release.

Validation and testing of an end-to-end service requires:

- Interfaces with suppliers, customers and partners
- Defined boundaries of the service to be tested, including process and organizational interfaces.

As well as covering the functionality of the components, testing examines their behaviour in conjunction with their intended use in the target business unit, service unit, deployment group or environment. To accomplish these tests it might be necessary to work with areas external to the service provider, such as public networks.

Testing supports the release and deployment process, ensuring the correct levels of testing have been undertaken, including the validation of the proposed service models as being 'fit for use' and 'fit for purpose' before authorization is given to enter service operation. Definitions are as follows:

- Fit for purpose means being able to deliver the required service utility. A service that is fit for purpose can meet all of its functional requirements.
- Fit for use means being able to deliver the required service warranty. A service that is fit for use is able to meet all of its operational requirements.

Information obtained during service validation and testing can be used to assess the performance of the live system as part of the change evaluation process.

4.3 VALUE TO THE BUSINESS (ST 4.5.3)

Service failures can harm the service provider's business and the customer's assets, and can result in outcomes such as damage to reputation, loss of money, loss of time, injury and even death.

Key values that the business and the customer gain from service testing and validation are confidence that a new or changed service will deliver the required value and outcomes, and an understanding of the risks.

4.4   POLICIES, PRINCIPLES AND BASIC CONCEPTS (ST 4.5.4)

Service validation and testing is driven by policies for:

- Service quality
- Risk
- Service transition (not covered in this publication)
- Release
- Change management.

4.4.1   Service quality policy

Senior leadership defines quality criteria for an organization, which is formalized in service strategy. The service provider should consider utility, warranty and service level metrics.

The four quality perspectives in service strategy are:

- Level of excellence
- Value for money
- Conformance to specification
- Meeting or exceeding expectations.

4.4.2   Risk policy

The level of validation and testing required will be determined in the risk policy. This can vary considerably depending on factors such as the business's appetite for risk, regulations and safety criticality.

The control required influences the amount of testing to be carried out regarding service level targets, utility and warranty (which covers availability, security, IT service continuity and capacity).

4.4.3 Release policy

The level and type of testing are influenced by type and frequency of releases.

4.4.4 Change management policy

The use of change windows can influence the testing that needs to be considered. For example, if there is a policy of 'substituting' a release package late in the change schedule, or if the scheduled release package is delayed, then additional testing may be required to assess this combination if there are dependencies.

4.4.5 Test models

Test models help to ensure consistency and repeatability, improving effectiveness and efficiency. Contents of a test model include a test plan ('What is to be tested?') and test scripts (including test conditions and expected results). To ensure the test model is repeatable it needs to be well structured.

Test models use service design and release plans to determine specific requirements. Separate test models can be created for the different types/stages of testing. Some examples of service test models are shown in Table 4.1.

Table 4.1 Examples of service test models

Test model	Objective/target deliverable	Test conditions based on
Service contract	Validate the service to make sure that customers can use it to deliver the value	Contract requirements, fit-for-purpose and fit-for-use criteria
Service requirements	Validate that the service provider can deliver the expected service	Service requirements and service acceptance criteria
Service level	Ensure that the service level requirements can be met in the production environment	Service level requirements, service level agreement, operational level agreement
Service	Ensure that the service provider is capable of operating and managing the service using the designed service model	Service model

Test model	Objective/target deliverable	Test conditions based on
Operations	Ensure that service operation teams can operate and support the service	Service model, service operation standards, processes and plans
Deployment release	Verify that the deployment team, tools and procedures can deploy the release correctly	Release and deployment design and plan
Deployment installation	Test that the release package can be correctly installed in target environment in the estimated time	Release and deployment design and plan
Deployment verification	Test that the deployment is completed and all assets and configurations are correct	Tests and audits of actual service assets and configurations

4.4.6   Validation and testing perspectives

The focus of validation and testing is to confirm that the service delivered fulfils all the agreed criteria, including the ability to deliver, deploy, use, manage and operate the service during its lifetime. The service design package (SDP) documents entry and exit criteria for each level and area of testing.

Perspectives to be considered include design of the service, technology, processes and measurements as well as documentation, skills and knowledge.

The service acceptance criteria and associated test plan are typically signed off by the stakeholders who agreed the service requirements.

4.4.7   Business user and customer perspective

The success of a service relies on the involvement of the people who have commissioned and will use the service. Acceptance testing by the business is included in the SDP. The importance of this to the business is that it enables:

- Measurement of acceptability of the service, including interfaces with the service provider
- Understanding of the resources needed to undertake the acceptance testing.

The importance of this to the service provider is that it:

- Maintains business involvement through the lifecycle, avoiding last-minute surprises
- Manages business perceptions of reliability and usability before the service goes live
- Provides acceptance test facilities to meet business requirements

■ Improves understanding of the links between acceptance testing and other business activities.

The period of acceptance testing allows the customer and users to become familiar with the new service well before live operation, reducing any initial resistance to change.

4.4.8 User testing – application, system and service

This testing reflects as closely as possible how the service will work in the live operational environment, checking that it provides the correct level of functionality and quality.

The areas that are covered include:

■ Required functionality
■ Changed business processes
■ Service management activities, such as contact with the service desk.

The scope and coverage of the tests are defined in the user test or user acceptance test plan.

4.4.9 Operations and service improvement perspective

Service acceptance checks that the following have been considered before deployment:

■ Technology and facilities
■ Support staff with requisite skills and knowledge
■ Supporting processes correctly resourced and in place (for example, the service desk)
■ Business and IT continuity
■ Access to documentation and the service knowledge management system (SKMS).

4.4.10 Levels of testing and testing models

Each service asset and component needs to be tested to ensure it meets the business, user and operational requirements before it is used in the live operational environment.

A re-usable test model is developed for each service model and associated deliverables, enabling regression-testing of specific releases for initial and subsequent deployments.

Figure 4.1 shows the V-model, which illustrates how some of the validation and testing activities can be undertaken early in the service lifecycle leading to increases in quality.

Figure 4.1 Example of service V-model

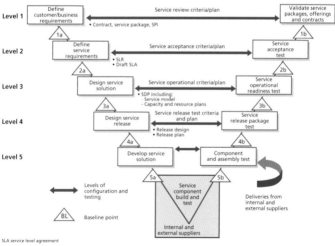

SLA service level agreement

SLR service level requirement

SPI service provider interface

The left side of the V-model shows stages of development; the right side shows related testing activity.

Development of the test model and the test-ware is undertaken at the same time as development of the designs and components to be tested.

The advantages of this approach are:

- Assumptions and omissions are identified at an early stage
- Early rectification of errors saves the cost of rework
- Test designs are based on the requirements, not on the solution
- Validation and testing activities are not constrained by tight timescales at the end of development.

The lowest level of component must be built before you start to execute tests. Testing is then conducted in reverse order following the right side of the V-model from bottom to top.

4.5   PROCESS ACTIVITIES, METHODS AND TECHNIQUES (ST 4.5.5)

The key activities undertaken in validation and testing are depicted in Figure 4.2.

The activities do not have to be undertaken sequentially; several can be done in parallel.

Figure 4.2 Example of a validation and testing process

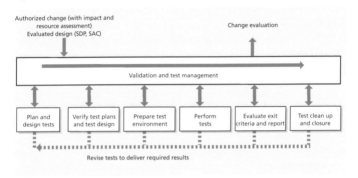

4.5.1   Validation and test management

This plans, monitors and controls the complete test lifecycle, including:

- Resource planning, activity prioritization and scheduling
- Management of incidents, problems, errors, non-conformances, risks and issues
- Monitoring and reporting, including collection, analysis and reporting on metrics
- Introduction of changes to reduce potential errors
- Capturing configuration baselines.

Proactive management of activities reduces delays and helps prevent dependencies from being created.

Control is achieved by the use of test metrics which show progress, provide information about earned value and determine the number of tests still required.

Estimation of test completion dates can be derived from good metrics, enabling the best testing to take place in the time available.

4.5.2 Plan and design tests

This starts early in the lifecycle and determines what should be considered in testing. It includes:

- Resourcing, including business and customer resources
- Hardware/networks
- Supporting services
- Schedule/milestones, including time allocation for review and acceptance of reports and other interim deliverables, and details for delivery and acceptance of products
- Budgets and financial requirements.

4.5.3 Verify test plan and test designs

This is undertaken to ensure that the test model provides:

- Appropriate test coverage for the level of risk
- Coverage of integration and interface aspects
- Examination of the accuracy and completeness of test scripts.

4.5.4 Prepare test environment

A test environment is a controlled environment used to test CIs, builds, IT services, processes etc.

Use build and test environment staff to create a suitable test environment with the assistance of the release and deployment management process. Take a configuration baseline once the initial test environment has been created.

4.5.5 Perform tests

Tests can be automated or executed manually. Record the tests to measure those that have run successfully and to raise incidents for any test failures, enabling the creation of resolutions or known errors.

Any updates will be retested, preferably by the same tester.

The deliverables from the activity are:

- Actual results with reference to the tests undertaken
- Outstanding problems, issues, risks etc. awaiting resolution
- Resolved problems, issues, risks etc. and associated changes
- Testing sign-off.

4.5.6 Evaluate exit criteria and report

This activity matches the actual result of the testing phase against the expected result and identifies any differences that would:

- Increase the risk to the business or service provider
- Change the projected value.

Examples of exit criteria are:

- The functionality provided matches the business requirements
- Quality requirements are met
- Configuration baselines are captured.

4.5.7 Test clean-up and closure

Ensure that test environments are cleaned up or initialized. Review the testing approach and identify any improvements that could be made.

4.6   TRIGGERS, INPUTS, OUTPUTS AND INTERFACES (ST 4.5.6)

Testing activities are scheduled in test, release or quality assurance plans.

Inputs include:

- **The SDP** Including the service model and service operation plans. Also incorporates service provider interface definitions and acceptance criteria for all levels of testing
- **RFCs** These instigate required changes to the environment within which the service functions or will function in future.

A key output is a report that is passed to change evaluation providing details of:

- The configuration baseline of the test environment
- Testing that was carried out and the results
- Risks identified when comparing expected and actual results.

This information is used to evaluate the progression of the service from before deployment, through early life support to normal operation.

Additional outputs are:

- Data, information and knowledge
- Test incident, problem and error records
- Ideas for any improvements to the testing process and service design outputs.

Successful testing requires interfaces with:

- Service design, to ensure designs are testable and support testing activities
- Service transition, to support all release and deployment steps

■ Continual service improvement, to provide feedback about failures and areas where improvement would be beneficial
■ Service operation, for handover of changed maintenance tests.

4.7   INFORMATION MANAGEMENT (ST 4.5.7)

Service validation and testing benefits from the ability to re-use tests. To facilitate re-use, the test management group is responsible for creating, cataloguing and maintaining test-ware. The use of CAST (computer-aided software testing) tools can also be beneficial.

Information is required on the following, to ensure realistic testing can take place:

■ **Test data** Including appropriate test conditions and environmental aspects
■ **Test environments** Wider impacts should be considered for significant change. The SKMS and configuration management system (CMS) assist the assessment which leads to:
  – Consequential update of the test data
  – Requirements for additional test data and environments
  – Redundancy of test data or environments
  – Testing restrictions because the test data and environment cannot be upgraded to reflect the changes
■ **Active maintenance of test data** To ensure clear distinction between test and live data, adherence to data protection regulations and use of known baselines.

4.8   CRITICAL SUCCESS FACTORS AND KEY PERFORMANCE INDICATORS (ST 4.5.8)

The efficiency and effectiveness of the process can be measured by identifying critical success factors (CSFs) for the process, each CSF being supported by key performance indicators (KPIs):

- **CSF** Understanding the different stakeholder perspectives that underpin effective risk management for the change impact assessment and test activities:
    - KPI Roles and responsibilities for impact assessment and test activities have been agreed and documented
    - KPI Increase in the number of new or changed services for which all roles and responsibilities for customers, users and service provider personnel have been agreed and documented
- **CSF** Building a thorough understanding of risks that have impacted or may impact successful service transition of services and releases:
    - KPI Reduction in the impact of incidents and errors for newly transitioned services
    - KPI Increased number of risks identified in service design or early in service transition compared to those detected during or after testing.

4.9   CHALLENGES AND RISKS

The most frequent challenges to effective testing are caused by a lack of respect for and understanding of the role of testing. Traditionally, testing has been starved of funding, resulting in:

- Inability to maintain a test environment and test data that match the live environment

- Insufficient staff, skills and testing tools to deliver adequate testing coverage
- Projects overrunning and allocated testing timeframes being squeezed to restore project go-live dates, but at the cost of quality
- Development of standard performance measures and measurement methods across projects and suppliers
- Projects and suppliers estimating delivery dates inaccurately and causing delays in scheduling service transition activities.

Risks include:

- Unclear expectations and objectives
- Lack of understanding of the risks resulting in testing that does not target the critical elements that need to be well controlled
- Resource shortages (e.g. users, support staff), that introduce delays and have an impact on other service transitions.

4.10   ROLES AND RESPONSIBILITIES (ST 6.4.9)

4.10.1 Service validation and testing process owner

Responsibilities include:

- Carrying out the generic process owner role for the service validation and testing process (see section 1.5 for more detail)
- Defining the overall test strategy for the organization
- Working with other process owners to ensure that there is an integrated approach to the design and implementation of change management, change evaluation, release and deployment management, and service validation and testing.

4.10.2 Service validation and testing process manager

Responsibilities include:

- Carrying out the generic process manager role for the service validation and testing process (see section 1.5 for more detail)
- Helping to design and plan testing conditions, test scripts and test data sets during the service design stage of the service lifecycle, to ensure appropriate and adequate coverage and control
- Allocating and overseeing test resources, ensuring that test policies are adhered to
- Verifying tests conducted by release and deployment management or other teams
- Managing test environment requirements
- Planning and managing support for service testing and validation tools and processes
- Providing management reporting on test progress, test outcomes, success rates, issues and risks.

It is important that this role is assigned to a different person from whoever is responsible for release and deployment management, to avoid conflicts of interest.

4.10.3 Service validation and testing practitioner

Responsibilities include:

- Conducting tests as defined in the test plans and designs, and documented in the SDP
- Recording, analysing, diagnosing, reporting and managing test events, incidents, problems and retest dependent on agreed criteria
- Administering test assets and components.

5 Release and deployment management

5.1 PURPOSE AND OBJECTIVES (ST 4.4.1)

The purpose of the release and deployment management process is to plan, schedule and control the build, test and deployment of releases, and to deliver the new functionality required by the business while protecting the integrity of existing services.

The objectives of release and deployment management include:

- Comprehensive plans that support customer and business change projects
- Releases that can be built, installed, tested and deployed efficiently and on time
- New or changed services that can meet agreed requirements
- Minimal unpredicted impact on services and on the IT organization.

5.2 SCOPE (ST 4.4.2)

The scope of release and deployment management includes the processes, systems and functions needed to package, build, test and deploy releases in order to establish the service specified in the service design package (SDP).

5.3 VALUE TO THE BUSINESS (ST 4.4.3)

Release and deployment management provides value to the business by:

- Delivering change faster, with optimized cost and risk
- Assuring that users are able to use new or changed services to support business goals
- Improving consistency and auditability of service transitions.

5.4   POLICIES, PRINCIPLES AND BASIC CONCEPTS (ST 4.4.4)

Release and deployment management policies help the organization achieve the correct balance between cost, service stability and agility. Release and deployment management policies help release and deployment management personnel to make decisions that support the overall objectives of the business.

5.4.1   Release unit and release package

A 'release unit' describes the portion of a service or IT infrastructure that is normally released as a single entity according to the organization's release policy. The unit may vary, depending on the type(s) or item(s) of service asset or service component such as software and hardware.

A 'release package' is a set of CIs that will be built, tested and deployed together as a single release. Each release will take the documented release units into account when designing the contents of the release package. The decision about what is an appropriate release unit is based on:

- Time and resources needed to build, test, distribute and implement
- Complexity of interfaces with other components
- Availability of resources in the test environment, and frequency and ease of change.

5.4.2   Deployment options

The components to be released, and the approach to be taken, are defined in the SDP. Common options include:

- ■ **'Big bang' vs phased**
  - Big bang The release is deployed to all users in one operation. It is often used when the same version must be in place in all locations.
  - Phased The release is deployed to different users, servers or places using a scheduled roll-out. It introduces the release in stages to reduce risk and make roll-back easier. It can also deploy part of the release (such as hardware upgrades) to all users and then deploy other parts.
- ■ **Push vs pull**
  - Push Deployment is managed from a central location. This is typically used for a big-bang deployment but can also be used with a phased approach.
  - Pull Users control the deployment timing. For example, virus signature updates may be pulled down to update a local PC at the user's convenience.
- ■ **Automated vs manual**
  - Automated This ensures repeatability, but takes time to design and implement. Many activities can be automated, including discovery, build, baselines, comparison of live to expected and updates to the configuration management system (CMS).
  - Manual This may not always be possible due to scalability and reliability. It must monitor and measure the impact and error rates.

Release and deployment models help to achieve consistency and repeatability. They include:

- How to build the release package and the target environments
- Exit and entry criteria for each stage, including handover activities
- Roles and responsibilities, template schedules and supporting systems and tools.

Each release and deployment model includes all activities needed to plan, package, build, test, deploy and implement the release.

5.5 PROCESS ACTIVITIES, METHODS AND TECHNIQUES (ST 4.4.5)

5.5.1 Planning

5.5.1.1 Release and deployment plans

Release and deployment plans should be based on overall service transition plans, use a release model, and be authorized by change management. They define:

- Scope and content of the release
- Risk assessment and risk profile for the release
- Stakeholders affected by the release, and approvers for the change request(s)
- Team responsible for release, resources needed, and approach to be taken.

5.5.1.2 Pass/fail criteria

Criteria must be defined for each authorization point, and must be published to stakeholders to set expectations. An example of a pass situation is when all tests have been completed successfully and the evaluation report and request for change (RFC) have been signed off.

Examples of fail situations include:

- There are insufficient resources to pass to next stage. For example, there is not enough money available or an automated build is not possible, so the risk is too high.
- Service operation does not have the required capabilities.
- The design does not conform to operational standards.
- The service acceptance criteria have not been met or there are incidents, problems or risks at higher than expected levels.

5.5.1.3 Build and test

Build and test planning includes:

- Developing build plans from the SDP and design specifications
- Establishing logistics, lead times and build times to create environments
- Scheduling activities and testing the procedures for build and test
- Assigning resources, roles and responsibilities
- Defining and agreeing entry and exit criteria for build and test.

The V-model (shown in Figure 4.1) represents the relationship between building and testing activities. At each build stage on the left, the testing personnel from the right are involved. For example, service acceptance tests are defined at the same time as service requirements.

The V-model is associated with the waterfall development lifecycle, but it can be used with other lifecycles such as prototyping and rapid application development. It includes five levels of build configuration, and corresponding tests, as shown in Table 5.1.

Table 5.1 The five levels of build configuration

Level	Deliverable	Testing
Level 1 Customer/business needs	Customer contract, based on service portfolio and service level package	**Service test and evaluation** The service can support business needs (i.e. it is fit for purpose and fit for use)
Level 2 Service requirements	Service capability and resources to deliver to service level agreement	**Service test** Service acceptance criteria can be met. The service can deliver the service level requirements
Level 3 Service solution	Solution or system required to deliver the capabilities, including management and operation	**Service operational readiness test** Integration and operation of the capability and resources. The organization and people are prepared
Level 4 Service release	Release package	**Service release test** Service components can be integrated and release can be installed, built and tested

Table continues

Table 5.1 *continued*

Level	Deliverable	Testing
Level 5 Component and assemblies	Components or assembly of components	**Component and assembly test** Component or assembly matches its specification

5.5.1.4   Planning pilots

Pilots test the service with some users before rolling it out to the whole user base. The scope of the pilot must be planned to provide enough testing with acceptable time and resources, and must include all stakeholders. Multiple pilots may be needed to support diverse organizations, or a range of different trialling options.

A pilot must collect feedback from users, customers, suppliers, and support staff. It also includes analysis of service desk calls, capacity, availability and other data on use and effectiveness.

Always roll back a pilot before the full deployment of the new service to ensure that a consistent release is deployed.

5.5.1.5   Planning release packaging and build

This includes developing mechanisms, plans and procedures for:

■ Verifying entry/exit criteria
■ Managing stakeholder change and communication, training people, transferring knowledge, and developing service management capability
■ Ensuring that agreements and contracts are in place
■ Agreeing schedules and developing procedures to build and deploy the release and manage licences

■ Converting users and systems (including any required data migrations).

5.5.1.6   Deployment planning
Planners should be able to answer the following questions:

■ What needs to be deployed? (The components and the business drivers for these)
■ Who are the users? (Any special language or training needs?)
■ Where are the users? (Are any users remote or mobile?)
■ Who else needs to be prepared in advance? (Service desk, support staff)
■ When does deployment need to be completed?
■ What is the current service provider capability? (Systems, infrastructure, capacity etc.)

5.5.1.7   Logistics and delivery planning
This stage includes planning for when and how each release unit or service component will be delivered. It requires planning for:

■ Lead times and how delays will be managed
■ Checking components on delivery and secure storage
■ Managing customs or other internationalization issues
■ Decommissioning redundant hardware, licences, contracts etc.
■ Resources needed for any parallel running.

5.5.1.8   Financial/commercial planning
Before the deployment starts it may be necessary to check:

■ Working capital – are sufficient funds available?
■ Contracts, licences, and intellectual property, including third-party software and rights to documentation
■ Funding for supporting services.

5.5.2 Preparation for build, test and deployment

Before authorizing the build and test stage:

- Carry out an independent evaluation to ensure the service will deliver the required outcomes (see Chapter 7)
- Assign people and other resources
- Carry out training for release, deployment, build and test teams.

5.5.3 Build and test

It is important to manage common services and infrastructure carefully, as they can have a significant impact. This includes build and test environments and management of configurations.

Configuration baselines must be recorded in the CMS before and after build, installation or deployment. Release packages must be placed in the definitive media library (DML) and must always be taken from the DML.

Procedures and documents are needed to manage the build and test. These include:

- Contracts, agreements, purchase requests, fulfilment, goods in etc.
- Health and safety guidelines, and security policies and procedures
- Management of licensing and intellectual property rights
- Acceptance and authorization
- Documentation for handover to service operation.

All CIs must be of a known quality, either from a catalogue of standard components or an RFC, raised to assess the CI and add it to the catalogue or accept it as an exception. CIs are acquired (possibly via procurement), recorded (via SACM) and checked. Verification of components includes:

- Establishing that they are genuine and have been properly acquired
- Checking that standard naming and labelling conventions have been applied
- Checking items against descriptions and documentation
- Checking that appropriate quality reviews have taken place
- Checking software for malicious additions such as viruses
- Ensuring that all changes have been approved by change management
- Ensuring appropriate use of the DML and CMS
- Managing the return of components that are not satisfactory.

The key activities to build a release package are:

- Assemble and integrate components in a controlled, reproducible way
- Create documentation for build and release
- Install and verify the release package and take a baseline
- Inform relevant parties that the release package is available for installation.

Dedicated environments are needed for release, build and test, and they must be controlled and managed using service management best practices. Automating the installation of systems and applications reduces dependency on people and streamlines the process.

5.5.4 Service testing and pilots

Testing is based on a test strategy and test model. New business or technical circumstances may need changes to acceptance criteria or service packages. These need service design input and business agreement, and include changes to testing to meet the new requirements.

There are many different types of test, including:

- **Service release test** To establish whether the release be installed, built and tested
- **Service operations readiness test** To find out if the service can be released, if the business is capable of using the service, and if the service teams are capable of operating the service:
  - Deployment readiness test Can the service be deployed correctly?
  - Service management test Can the live service performance be measured, monitored and reported on?
  - Service operations test Can the service be operated?
  - Service level test Can service level requirements be delivered?
  - User test Can users access and use the service correctly?
  - Service provider interface test Are interfaces working correctly?
  - Deployment verification test Was everything deployed correctly to each target?
- **Service rehearsal** A simulation of as much of the service as possible in a practice session, just before deployment. It can be time-consuming and extensive, but may identify errors or unworkable procedures. It typically uses a full Plan-Do-Check-Act cycle for a one-day rehearsal
- **Pilot** Real users and operations, but involving a limited number of people. It checks enough of the service to verify both utility and warranty. It includes training, documentation and all stakeholder interaction.

5.5.5 Plan and prepare for deployment, and perform transfer, deployment and retirement

These stages include preparing for organizational change, assigning deployment activities to specific people, and actually carrying out the deployment. Figure 5.1 shows a typical set of deployment activities.

Figure 5.1 Example of a set of deployment activities

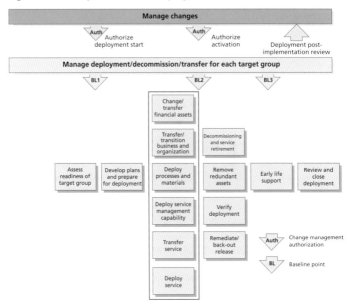

5.5.6   Verify deployment

During this stage, checks are made to verify the deployment:

- Does the new configuration baseline match the planned configuration?
- Are documentation updates correct?
- Are required communication and learning materials ready for distribution?
- Have roles been assigned? Are people prepared to operate and use the service? Do they have the information they need?
- Are measurement and reporting in place?

5.5.7   Early life support

During this stage, checks are carried out to ensure that all agreed service levels are being met. Performance data is collected and compared with targets. Service reports are created and issues are addressed. Early life support does not end until the agreed exit criteria have been met. These typically include:

- Users can use the service effectively and efficiently for business activities
- Service and process owners can manage and operate the service as agreed
- Progress is being made towards delivering the expected benefits
- Service level agreements (SLAs) are signed off and service levels are being consistently achieved
- Training, knowledge transfer, documentation and deliverables are signed off.

Note: Early life support is sometimes confused with provision of additional technical support for managing incidents and problems. Although this may be done during early life support, the key aspect is collecting performance data to verify that the service is able to meet all agreed service levels.

5.5.8 Review and close deployment, review and close service transition

The final stages are formal reviews to ensure that:

- All outstanding issues have been documented and addressed
- Opportunities for improvement have been captured.

5.6 TRIGGERS, INPUTS, OUTPUTS AND INTERFACES (ST 4.4.6)

Release and deployment always starts with an approved RFC.

Inputs include:

- One or more authorized RFCs
- The SDP, including service model and service acceptance criteria
- Service management plans and standards
- Release policy and release design from service design
- Release and deployment models, and template plans
- Entry and exit criteria for each stage of release and deployment.

Outputs include:

- New, changed or retired services
- Release and deployment plan

- Updated service catalogue and new or changed documentation
- Updates to service level packages, service models, SLAs, operational level agreements and contracts
- New, tested service capability, including organizational changes, applications, data, infrastructure, environment etc.
- Updated configuration management database (CMDB) with full audit trail of new or changed CIs
- Updated service management plans (e.g. capacity plan, continuity plan)
- Service transition report.

Interfaces include:

- Design coordination
- Transition planning and support
- Change management
- Service asset and configuration management
- Service validation and testing.

5.7   INFORMATION MANAGEMENT (ST 4.4.7)

Release and deployment management makes extensive use of the CMS, including updates for:

- New or changed CIs, including ownership, status, attributes and relationships
- New or changed locations or users
- Plans and records for installation, build, logistics, delivery, validation and testing, deployment, and training
- Known errors.

5.8   CRITICAL SUCCESS FACTORS AND KEY PERFORMANCE INDICATORS (ST 4.4.8)

The efficiency and effectiveness of the process can be measured by identifying critical success factors (CSFs) for the process, each CSF being supported by key performance indicators (KPIs):

- **CSF** Ensuring integrity of a release package and its constituent components throughout the transition activities:
  - KPI Reduced number of CMS and DML audit failures related to releases
  - KPI Reduced number of deployments from sources other than the DML
- **CSF** Ensuring that the new or changed service is capable of delivering the agreed utility and warranty:
  - KPI Reduced variance from service performance required by customers
  - KPI Number of incidents against the service (low and reducing).

5.9   CHALLENGES AND RISKS (ST 4.4.9)

Challenges include:

- Developing standard measures across many projects and suppliers
- Managing schedule delays caused by projects and suppliers
- Understanding diverse stakeholder perspectives
- Understanding risks and building a risk management culture.

Risks include:

- Poorly defined scope and understanding of dependencies
- Staff who are not dedicated and have other responsibilities
- Inadequate management, policies or leadership

- Insufficient finance or delays in provision of money
- Insufficient control of changes, or poor implementation or back-out plans
- Technology limitations or issues.

5.10   TYPICAL DAY-TO-DAY ACTIVITIES PERFORMED BY SERVICE OPERATION (SO 5.12.3)

Release and deployment management is undertaken in service transition, but there are some aspects that service operation staff are involved with on a day-to-day basis. These include:

- Actual implementation actions regarding the deployment of new releases, under the direction of release and deployment management, where they relate to service operation components or services
- Participation in the planning stages of major new releases to advise on service operation issues
- The physical handling of CIs from and to the DML as required to fulfil their operational roles – while adhering to relevant release and deployment management procedures, such as ensuring that all items are properly booked out and back in
- Participation in activities to back out unsuccessful releases when these occur.

5.11   ROLES AND RESPONSIBILITIES (ST 6.4.8)

The role of the release and deployment manager is described here. The role of the service test manager is described in section 4.10. These roles must be undertaken by different people to ensure that testing is independent. Both roles report to the service transition manager.

5.11.1 Release and deployment management process owner

Responsibilities include:

- Carrying out the generic process owner role for the release and deployment management process (see section 1.5 for more detail)
- Designing release models and workflows
- Working with other process owners to ensure there is an integrated approach to all aspects of service transition.

5.11.2 Release and deployment manager

Responsibilities include:

- Carrying out the generic process manager role for the release and deployment management process (see section 1.5 for more detail)
- Planning and coordinating all resources needed to build, test and deploy each release, including resources from other functions such as technical management or application management
- Planning and managing support for release and deployment management tools and processes
- Ensuring that change authorization is provided before any activity that requires this
- Coordinating interfaces between release and deployment management and other processes, especially change management, SACM, and service validation and testing.

5.11.3 Release packaging and build practitioner

The release packaging and build practitioner typically reports to the release and deployment manager and has the following responsibilities:

- Establishing the knowledge, information, hardware, software and infrastructure needed for the release
- Building and testing the final release (prior to independent testing)
- Reporting outstanding known errors and providing input to final sign-off.

5.11.4 Deployment practitioner

Deployment staff deal with the final physical delivery of the service. They coordinate documentation and communications, and provide technical and application guidance and support.

5.11.5 Early life support practitioner

Early life support starts a long time before the service enters operational status. Early life support staff are responsible for:

- Ensuring delivery and quality of user and support documentation
- Embedding all activities required for the service to be operated and maintained
- Providing initial performance reporting and risk assessment of performance
- Providing initial support for incidents and errors.

6   Request fulfilment

6.1   PURPOSE AND OBJECTIVES (SO 4.3.1)

Request fulfilment is the process for dealing with service requests from the users through their lifecycle.

The objectives of the request fulfilment process are to:

- Maintain user and customer satisfaction by handling all service requests in an efficient and professional manner
- Provide a channel for users to request and receive standard services for which there is a predefined authorization and qualification process
- Provide information to users and customers about the availability of services and the procedure for obtaining them
- Source and deliver the components of requested standard services (e.g. licences and software media)
- Assist with general information, complaints or comments.

6.2   SCOPE (SO 4.3.2)

Some organizations deal with service requests through their incident management process (and tools), with service requests being handled as a particular type of 'incident'. However, there is a significant difference between an incident – usually an unplanned event – and a service request, which is something that should be planned. The process needed to fulfil a request varies depending upon exactly what is being requested, but it can usually be broken down into a set of activities that have to be performed.

Therefore, in an organization where large numbers of service requests have to be handled, and where the actions to be taken to fulfil those requests are very varied or specialized, it may be appropriate to handle service requests as a completely separate work stream. Ultimately it is up to each organization to decide and document which service requests it handles through the request fulfilment process and which have to go through other processes.

6.3   VALUE TO THE BUSINESS AND SERVICE LIFECYCLE (SO 4.3.3)

The value of request fulfilment includes:

- Quick and effective access to standard services; this can improve business productivity and/or quality
- A less bureaucratic system for requesting and receiving access to existing or new services, reducing the cost of providing these services
- Where fulfilment is centralized, having more control over services can reduce costs as supplier negotiation is also centralized and support costs are lower.

6.4   POLICIES, PRINCIPLES AND BASIC CONCEPTS (SO 4.3.4)

Examples of request fulfilment policies include:

- The request fulfilment activities follow a predefined process flow or model which includes all stages needed to fulfil the request, the individuals or support groups involved, target timescales and escalation paths

- The ownership of service requests resides with a centralized function; for example, the service desk, which monitors, escalates, despatches and may also fulfil the request
- Service requests that impact CIs are usually fulfilled by implementing a standard change
- All requests are logged, controlled, coordinated, promoted and managed throughout their lifecycle via a single system
- All requests are authorized before activities are undertaken to fulfil them.

6.4.1 Request models

Service request models (which typically include one or more standard changes in order to complete fulfilment activities) are defined, to ensure that frequently used service requests are handled consistently and meet agreed service levels.

6.4.2 Menu selection

Request fulfilment offers great opportunities for self-help. Users are offered a self-help menu from which they can select requests and provide details.

6.4.3 Request status tracking

Track requests throughout their lifecycle to support proper handling of requests and reporting on their status. Within the request fulfilment system, status codes may be linked to requests to indicate where they are in relation to the lifecycle. Examples include: in review, suspended, awaiting authorization, rejected, cancelled, in progress, completed, and closed.

6.4.4   Financial approval

The cost of providing the service should first be established and submitted to the user for approval within their management chain. In some cases there may be a need for additional compliance approval, or wider business approval.

6.4.5   Coordination of fulfilment activities

Fulfilment activity depends upon the type of service request. Simple requests may be completed by the service desk, while others are forwarded to specialist groups and/or suppliers for fulfilment. The service desk monitors progress and keeps users informed throughout, regardless of the actual fulfilment source.

6.5   PROCESS ACTIVITIES, METHODS AND TECHNIQUES (SO 4.3.5)

6.5.1   Request receipt, logging and validation

Fulfilment work on service requests should not begin until a formalized request has been received, typically from the service desk. All service requests must be fully logged. Service request records include:

- Unique reference number
- Request categorization, urgency, impact and prioritization
- Date and time recorded, fulfilled and closed
- Name, ID, department and location of the person and/or group making the request
- Method of notification (for example, telephone, web interface, RFC, email, in person)
- Budget centre in case a charge is incurred
- Description of request

- Request status
- Related CIs
- Support group or person to which the service request is allocated.

6.5.2 Request categorization and prioritization

Requests can be categorized in several ways: for example, by service, activity, type, function or CI type.

Prioritization is determined by taking into account both the urgency of the request (how quickly the business needs to have it fulfilled) and the level of impact it is causing. The factors contributing to impact levels are as follows: the number of services impacted; the number of users or business units impacted; whether the requester is at an executive level; the level of financial gain or loss; the effect on business reputation; and regulatory or legislative requirements. A table can be generated for determining priority, as for incident management.

There may also be occasions when, because of particular business expediency, normal priority levels have to be overridden. Some organizations may also recognize 'VIPs', whose service requests are handled as a higher priority than normal.

6.5.3 Request authorization

No work to fulfil a request should occur until it is authorized. Requests can be authorized via the service desk or by having pre-authorized requests. Alternatively, authorization may need to come from other sources; these could include access management, to determine whether the requester is authorized to make the request, or financial management, to authorize any charges or costs associated with fulfilling the request.

Service requests that cannot be authorized are returned to the requester with the reason for the rejection. The request record is also updated to indicate the rejection status.

6.5.4   Request review

The request is reviewed to determine the appropriate group to fulfil it. As requests are reviewed, escalated and acted upon, the request record is updated to reflect the current request status.

6.5.5   Request model execution

A request model documents a standard process flow, setting out the roles and responsibilities for fulfilling each request type to ensure that the fulfilment activities are repeatable and consistent. The relevant request model is chosen and executed for each service request.

Request models may be described as process steps and activities that are stored as reference documents in the service knowledge management system (SKMS). Alternatively they may be stored through specialized configurations within automated workflow tools or through code elements and configurations as part of web-based self-help solutions.

Any service requests that impact CIs in the live environment are authorized through change management, typically as standard changes.

6.5.6   Request closure

Fulfilled service requests are referred back to the service desk for closure. Having checked that the user is satisfied with the outcome, the service desk also ensures that any financial requirements are complete, confirms that the request categorization was correct (or if not, corrects it), carries out a user satisfaction survey, chases any outstanding documentation and formally closes the request.

6.6   TRIGGERS, INPUTS, OUTPUTS AND INTERFACES (SO 4.3.6)

The trigger for request fulfilment is the user submitting a service request, either via the service desk or using a self-help facility. This often involves selection from a portfolio of available request types.

Inputs include:

- Work requests
- Authorization forms
- Service requests
- RFCs
- Requests from various sources such as phone calls, web interfaces or email
- Requests for information.

Outputs include:

- Authorized or rejected service requests
- Request fulfilment status reports
- Fulfilled, updated, closed and cancelled service requests
- Incidents (rerouted)
- RFCs and standard changes
- Asset and CI updates
- Updated request records.

The primary interfaces are concerned with requesting services and their subsequent deployment:

- **Financial management for IT services** Interfaces may be needed if costs for fulfilling requests need to be reported and recovered
- **Service catalogue management** Links with request fulfilment to ensure that requests are well known to users and linked with services in the catalogue that they support
- **Release and deployment management** Some requests are for the deployment of new or upgraded components that can be automatically deployed
- **Service asset and configuration management** Once deployed, the configuration management system (CMS) has to be updated to reflect changes that may have been made as part of fulfilment activities
- **Change management** Where a change is required to fulfil a request, it is logged as an RFC and progressed through change management
- **Incident and problem management** Requests may come in via the service desk and may initially be handled through the incident management process
- **Access management** Ensures that those making requests are authorized to do so in accordance with the information security policy.

6.7   INFORMATION MANAGEMENT (SO 4.3.7)

Request fulfilment is dependent on information from the following sources:

- **RFCs** The request fulfilment process may be initiated by an RFC, usually if the service request relates to a CI
- **Service portfolio** Enables the scope of agreed service requests to be identified

- **Security policies** Prescribe controls to be executed or adhered to, such as ensuring that the requester is authorized to access the service
- **Authorized approvers** People authorized to approve the requests.

Service requests contain information about which service is being asked for, who requested and authorized it, the process used to fulfil the request, the assignee and any actions, date and time of logging, and subsequent actions and closure details.

6.8 CRITICAL SUCCESS FACTORS AND KEY PERFORMANCE INDICATORS (SO 4.3.8)

The efficiency and effectiveness of the process can be measured by identifying critical success factors (CSFs) for the process, each CSF being supported by key performance indicators (KPIs):

- **CSF** Requests must be fulfilled in an efficient and timely manner that is aligned to agreed service level targets for each type of request:
  - KPI The mean elapsed time for handling each type of service request
  - KPI The number and percentage of service requests completed within agreed target times
  - KPI Breakdown of service requests at each stage (e.g. logged, work in progress, closed)
  - KPI Percentage of service requests closed by the service desk without reference to other levels of support (often referred to as 'first point of contact')
  - KPI Number and percentage of service requests resolved remotely or through automation, without the need for a visit

- – KPI Total numbers of requests (as a control measure)
- – KPI The average cost per type of service request
- ■ **CSF** Only authorized requests are fulfilled:
  - – KPI Percentage of service requests fulfilled that were appropriately authorized
  - – KPI Number of incidents related to security threats from request fulfilment activities
- ■ **CSF** User satisfaction must be maintained:
  - – KPI Level of user satisfaction with the handling of service requests (as measured in some form of satisfaction survey)
  - – KPI Total number of incidents related to request fulfilment activities
  - – KPI Size of the current backlog of outstanding service requests.

6.9   CHALLENGES AND RISKS (SO 4.3.9)

Challenges include:

- ■ Clearly defining the type of requests to be handled by the request fulfilment process
- ■ Establishing self-help capabilities at the front end that allow the users to interface successfully with the request fulfilment process
- ■ Agreeing and establishing service level targets
- ■ Agreeing the costs for fulfilling requests
- ■ Putting in place agreements for which services are standardized and who is authorized to request them
- ■ Making information easily accessible about which requests are available

- Making requests follow a predefined standard fulfilment procedure
- The high impact of request fulfilment on user satisfaction.

Risks include:

- Poorly defined scope, where people are unclear about what the process is expected to handle
- Poorly designed or implemented user interfaces, meaning that users have difficulty raising requests
- Badly designed or operated back-end fulfilment processes that are incapable of dealing with the volume or nature of the requests
- Inadequate monitoring capabilities, meaning that accurate metrics cannot be gathered.

6.10 ROLES AND RESPONSIBILITIES (SO 6.7.7)

6.10.1 Request fulfilment process owner

Responsibilities include:

- Carrying out the generic process owner role for the request fulfilment process (see section 1.5)
- Designing request fulfilment models and workflows
- Working with other process owners to ensure there is an integrated approach across request fulfilment, incident management, event management, access management and problem management.

6.10.2 Request fulfilment process manager

Responsibilities include:

- Carrying out the generic process manager role for the request fulfilment process (see section 1.5)
- Planning and managing support for request fulfilment tools and processes, and coordinating interfaces with other service management processes
- Assisting with identification of suitable staffing levels to deliver request fulfilment activities and services
- Ensuring all authorized service requests are being fulfilled on a timely basis, in line with service level targets
- Representing request fulfilment activities at change advisory board (CAB) meetings
- Overseeing feedback from customers and reviewing request fulfilment activities for consistency, accuracy and effectiveness in order to proactively seek improvements.

6.10.3 Request fulfilment analyst

Responsibilities include:

- Providing a single point of contact and end-to-end responsibility to ensure submitted service requests have been processed
- Providing an initial triage of service requests to determine which IT resources will be engaged to fulfil them
- Communicating service requests to other IT resources that will be involved in fulfilling them
- Escalating service requests in line with established service level targets
- Ensuring service requests are appropriately logged.

7 Change evaluation

7.1 PURPOSE AND OBJECTIVES (ST 4.6.1)

The purpose of the change evaluation process is to provide a consistent and standardized means of determining the performance of a service change in the context of likely impacts on business outcomes, and on existing and proposed services and IT infrastructure. The actual performance of a change is assessed against its predicted performance. Risks and issues related to the change are identified and managed.

The objectives of change evaluation are to:

- Set stakeholder expectations correctly and provide effective and accurate information to change management to make sure that changes which adversely affect service capability and introduce risk are not transitioned unchecked
- Evaluate the intended effects of a service change and as many of the unintended effects as is reasonably practical given capacity, resource and organizational constraints
- Provide good-quality outputs so that change management can expedite an effective decision about whether or not a service change is to be authorized.

7.2 SCOPE (ST 4.6.2)

Every change must be authorized by a suitable change authority at various points in its lifecycle; for example, before build and test, before it is checked into the definitive media library (DML), and before it is deployed to the live environment. Evaluation is required before each of these authorizations, to provide the change authority with advice and guidance.

This change evaluation process describes a formal evaluation that is suitable for use when significant changes are being evaluated. Each organization must decide which changes should use this formal change evaluation, and which can be evaluated as part of the change management process. This is normally documented in the change models used to manage each type of change.

7.3   VALUE TO THE BUSINESS (ST 4.6.3)

Change evaluation is, by its very nature, concerned with value. Specifically, effective change evaluation establishes the use made of resources in terms of delivered benefit, and this information allows a more accurate focus on value in future service development and change management. There is a great deal of intelligence that continual service improvement can take from change evaluation to inform future improvements to the process of change and the predictions and measurement of service change performance.

7.4   POLICIES, PRINCIPLES AND BASIC CONCEPTS (ST 4.6.4)

Examples of change evaluation policies include:

- Service designs or service changes are evaluated before being transitioned
- Every change must be evaluated, but because only significant changes go through the formal change evaluation process, criteria must be defined to identify which changes are in its scope
- Change evaluation identifies risks and issues to the service being changed and any other services
- Any deviation between predicted and actual performance is managed by the customer or customer representative by:

- Accepting the change, even though actual performance is different from what was predicted
- Rejecting the change
- Requiring a new change to be implemented with revised predicted performance agreed in advance.
  No other outcomes of change evaluation are allowed.

The unintended as well as the intended effects of a change need to be identified and their consequences understood and considered.

An evaluation report, or interim evaluation report, is provided to change management to facilitate decision-making at each point at which authorization is required.

The change evaluation process uses the Plan-Do-Check-Act (PDCA) model to ensure consistency across all evaluations. Each evaluation is planned and then carried out in multiple stages, the results of the evaluation are checked and actions are taken to resolve any issues found.

7.5   PROCESS ACTIVITIES, METHODS AND TECHNIQUES (ST 4.6.5)

Key terms used in change evaluation are defined in Table 7.1.

Figure 7.1 shows the change evaluation process with inputs and outputs.

7.5.1   Evaluation plan

Change evaluation is carried out from several different perspectives to help identify unintended as well as intended effects.

Table 7.1 Key terms used in change evaluation

Actual performance	The performance achieved following a service change
Capacity	The organization's ability to maintain service capability in defined circumstances
Constraint	Limits on an organization's capacity
Countermeasures	Mitigation that is implemented to reduce risk
Deviations report	A report identifying differences between predicted and actual performance
Evaluation plan	The outcome of the evaluation planning exercise – a plan to perform the evaluation
Evaluation report	A report passed to change management at the end of evaluation. It includes risk profile, deviations report, qualification or validation statements (if applicable) and recommendations
Interim evaluation report	A report passed to change management before the end of evaluation, if there is an unacceptable level of risk
Performance	The utilities and warranties of a service
Performance model	A representation of the performance of a service
Residual risk	The remaining risk after countermeasures have been deployed

Resource	The normal requirements of an organization to maintain service capability
Risk	A function of the likelihood and negative impact of a service not performing as expected
Service capability	Ability of a service to perform as required
Service change	A change to an existing service or the introduction of a new service (a formal definition of service change can be found in section 2.4.1)
Service design package (SDP)	Defines the service and provides a plan of service changes over the next period (for example, 12 months). It includes acceptance criteria and predicted performances
Test plan and results	A test plan is a response to an impact assessment. It typically specifies, for example, how the change will be tested, what records will be created and where they will be stored. It may also include plans for qualification and validation. Test results represent the actual performance following change implementation

Figure 7.1 Change evaluation process flow

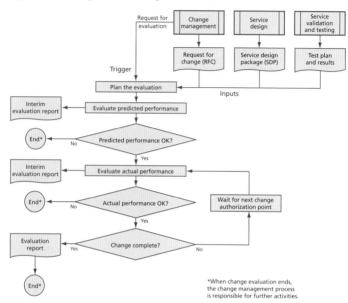

7.5.2   Understanding intended and unintended effects of a change

The SDP is analysed to understand the change and the expected benefits. Documentation should make the intended effects clear and include specific measures to determine the effectiveness of the change. Note that some of the intended effects may be detrimental to the service; for example, introducing Sarbanes-Oxley compliant procedures may add extra steps and costs.

Table 7.2 Factors to consider when assessing the effects of a service change

Factor	Evaluation of service design
S – Service provider capability	Ability of the service provider or service to perform as required
T – Tolerance	Ability or capacity of a service to absorb the change
O – Organizational setting	Ability of the organization to accept the change
R – Resources	Availability of skilled and knowledgeable people, finance, infrastructure, applications and other resources needed to run the service after the change
M – Modelling and measurement	Extent to which predicted performance matches actual behaviour
P – People	The effect of the change on the people
U – Use	Will the service be fit for use? Can warranties be met?
P – Purpose	Will the service be fit for purpose? Can required performance be supported? Will constraints be removed as planned?

Unintended effects of the change must be identified wherever possible. This may involve discussions with stakeholders and attempts to understand the full impact of the change. Table 7.2 shows factors to be taken into account when considering the predicted effect of a service change.

7.5.3 Evaluation of predicted and actual performance

A risk assessment is carried out, based on customer requirements (including acceptance criteria) and predicted performance. If this risk assessment shows unacceptable risks, then an interim evaluation report is created to warn change management, and evaluation activity stops until change management makes a decision.

After the change has been implemented, a report on actual performance is received from operations staff (or early life support) and another risk assessment is carried out. If this risk assessment shows unacceptable risks, then an interim evaluation report is created to warn change management, and evaluation activity stops until change management makes a decision.

In each case, the risk assessment is based on analysing threats and weaknesses. Risk is calculated as likelihood of event multiplied by impact of event. Risk mitigation may be used to reduce the risk, resulting in a residual risk.

If risks are acceptable, then no interim evaluation report is produced and further analysis is carried out to create an evaluation report. This contains:

- **Deviations report** Comparing actual with predicted performance
- **Risk profile** Showing the residual risk
- **Qualification statement or validation statement (if appropriate)** A formal statement showing compliance with regulations, such as those required in defence and pharmaceutical

industries. Services and applications may be validated;
infrastructure and operating environments may be qualified

■ **Recommendation** Advising change management whether to
accept or reject the change.

Note: An interim evaluation report is produced before the end of
evaluation if risks are seen as unacceptable. An evaluation report
is only produced at the end of evaluation if risks are acceptable.

7.6   TRIGGERS, INPUTS, OUTPUTS AND INTERFACES (ST 4.6.6)

The trigger for change evaluation is receipt of a request for
evaluation from change management.

Inputs include:

■ SDP, including service charter and service acceptance criteria
■ Change proposal
■ RFC, change record and detailed change documentation
■ Discussions with stakeholders
■ Test results and report.

Outputs are:

■ Interim evaluation report(s) for change management
■ Evaluation report for change management.

The change evaluation process must be tightly integrated with
change management. There should be clear agreement on which
types of change are subject to formal evaluation, and the time
required for this evaluation must be included in the overall
planning for the change. Change management provides the
trigger for change evaluation, and the evaluation report must be

delivered to change management in time for the CAB (or other change authority) to use it to assist in their decision-making.

Change evaluation requires information about the service, which is supplied by service design coordination in the form of an SDP.

Change evaluation may need to work with service level management or business relationship management to ensure a full understanding of the impact of any issues identified, and to obtain use of user or customer resources if these are needed to help perform the evaluation.

Change evaluation requires information from the service validation and testing process, and must coordinate activities with this process to ensure that required inputs are available in sufficient time.

7.7   INFORMATION MANAGEMENT (ST 4.6.7)

Much of the information required for change evaluation should be available from the service knowledge management system (SKMS). All evaluation reports should be checked into the CMS and soft-copy versions of the reports stored in the SKMS.

7.8   CRITICAL SUCCESS FACTORS AND KEY PERFORMANCE INDICATORS (ST 4.6.8)

The efficiency and effectiveness of the process can be measured by identifying critical success factors (CSFs) for the process, each CSF being supported by key performance indicators (KPIs):

- **CSF** Stakeholders have a good understanding of the expected performance of new and changed services:
  - KPI Reduced number of incidents for new or changed services caused by failure to deliver expected utility or warranty

- KPI Increased stakeholder satisfaction with new or changed services as measured in customer surveys
- **CSF** Change management has good-quality evaluations to help make correct decisions:
  - KPI Increased percentage of evaluations delivered by agreed times
  - KPI Reduced number of changes that have to be backed out due to unexpected errors or failures.

7.9   CHALLENGES AND RISKS (ST 4.6.9)

Challenges include:

- Developing standard performance measures and measurement methods
- Inaccuracy of information supplied by suppliers and projects
- Understanding different stakeholder perspectives
- Managing risk as it affects the overall organization, communicating the approach to risk, and encouraging a risk management culture
- Measuring variation in predictions during and after transition and demonstrating improvement.

Risks include:

- Lack of clear criteria for when change evaluation is used
- Unrealistic expectations of the time required for change evaluation
- Change evaluation personnel with insufficient experience or organizational authority to be able to influence change authorities
- Projects and suppliers estimating delivery dates inaccurately and causing delays in scheduling change evaluation activities.

7.10   ROLES AND RESPONSIBILITIES (ST 6.4.10)

7.10.1 Change evaluation process owner

Responsibilities include:

- Carrying out the generic process owner role for the change evaluation process (see section 1.5)
- Working with other process owners to ensure that there is an integrated approach to service management.

7.10.2 Change evaluation process manager

Responsibilities include:

- Carrying out the generic process manager role for the change evaluation process (see section 1.5)
- Planning and coordinating all resources needed to evaluate changes
- Ensuring that change evaluation delivers evaluation reports and interim evaluation reports in time to ensure that change authorities are able to use them to support their decision-making.

7.10.3 Change evaluation practitioner

Responsibilities include:

- Using the service design and the release package to develop an evaluation plan as input to service validation and testing
- Establishing risks and issues associated with all aspects of the service transition (for example, through risk workshops)
- Creating an evaluation report as input to change management.

8 Knowledge management

8.1 PURPOSE AND OBJECTIVES (ST 4.7.1)

The ability to deliver a quality service or process relies on people understanding the circumstances, options, consequences and benefits of the situation; in other words, their knowledge.

The purpose of knowledge management is to enable organizations to improve the quality of decision-making by ensuring that reliable and secure information and data are available.

The objectives of knowledge management are to:

- Improve the quality of management decision-making by ensuring that reliable and secure knowledge, information and data are available throughout the service lifecycle.
- Enable the service provider to be more efficient and improve the quality of the service; increase satisfaction; and reduce the cost of the service by obviating the need to rediscover knowledge.
- Ensure that staff have a clear and common understanding of the value that their services provide to customers and the ways in which benefits are realized from the use of those services.
- Maintain a service knowledge management system (SKMS) that provides controlled access to knowledge, information and data that is appropriate for each audience.
- Gather, analyse, store, share, use and maintain knowledge, information and data throughout the service provider organization.

8.2   SCOPE (ST 4.7.2)

The scope of knowledge management extends across the lifecycle and is referenced throughout ITIL. It includes oversight of the management of knowledge, and the information and data from which that knowledge is derived.

The scope of knowledge management does **not** include the capture, maintenance and use of service asset configuration data. These activities remain under the control and management of service asset and configuration management.

8.3   VALUE TO THE BUSINESS (ST 4.7.3)

Knowledge management is especially significant within service transition. For example, it is important in:

- Transitioning knowledge to users, service desk and suppliers by means of training
- Making everyone aware of discontinued versions of whatever is to be released
- The establishment of acceptable risk and confidence levels associated with the transition.

Effective knowledge management is a powerful asset for all roles across the service lifecycle.

Implementation of an SKMS helps reduce the cost of maintaining and managing services by increasing the efficiency of operational procedures and reducing risks that arise from the lack of proper mechanisms.

8.4   POLICIES, PRINCIPLES AND BASIC CONCEPTS (ST 4.7.4)

8.4.1   Knowledge management policies

Knowledge management policies are required to guide all staff in the behaviours needed to make it effective. Policy statements will be very dependent on the culture of the organization, but typically might include the following:

- The knowledge and information needed to support the services must be stored in a way that allows them to be accessed by all staff when and where they are needed
- All policies, plans and processes must be reviewed at least once per year
- All knowledge and information must be created, reviewed, approved, maintained, controlled and disposed of following a formal documented process.

8.4.2   Data-to-Information-to-Knowledge-to-Wisdom structure

The Data-to-Information-to-Knowledge-to-Wisdom structure (DIKW) is shown in Figure 8.1.

Knowledge management uses the terms 'data', 'information', 'knowledge' and 'wisdom' with the following meanings:

- **Data** Is facts about events. Most organizations capture massive amounts of data, some of which is stored in structured databases, such as service management, configuration management system (CMS) and databases.
- **Information** Comes from providing a context to data. Information is typically stored in semi-structured formats such as in documents, spreadsheets and email. Knowledge

management facilitates capture, query, finding, re-using and learning from information, so that mistakes are not repeated and work is not duplicated.

- **Knowledge** Is composed of tacit experiences, ideas and insights, values and judgements of individuals. People gain knowledge both from their own expertise and that of their peers as well as from the analysis of information and data. Knowledge is dynamic and context-based. Knowledge transforms information into a format that is easy to use. This is achieved by use of previously collected experiences, awareness and anticipation.
- **Wisdom** Uses application and contextual awareness to provide judgement.

Figure 8.1 The flow from data to wisdom

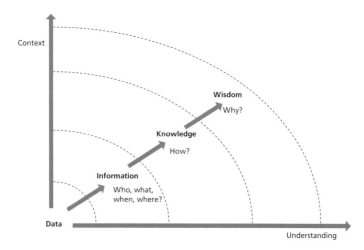

8.4.3 The service knowledge management system

Specifically within IT service management, knowledge management is focused within the SKMS. Underpinning this knowledge is a considerable quantity of data and information, held in the CMS. Figure 8.2 shows that the SKMS is a broader concept than the CMS, and includes a much wider base of knowledge, such as:

- The experience of staff
- Records of peripheral matters such as weather reports and organization performance
- Requirements, abilities and expectations of suppliers or users.

Figure 8.2 Relationship of the CMDB, the CMS and the SKMS

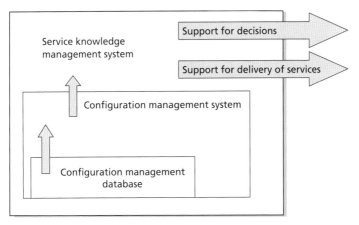

8.5   PROCESS ACTIVITIES, METHODS AND TECHNIQUES (ST 4.7.5)

8.5.1   Knowledge management strategy

There should be as wide a span as practicable for knowledge management to incorporate anyone likely to be able to contribute to or benefit from knowledge management.

Specifically, knowledge management identifies and plans for the capture of relevant knowledge and the information and data that support it.

8.5.2   Knowledge transfer

During the lifecycle an organization needs to focus on retrieving, sharing and using its knowledge through problem-solving, dynamic learning, strategic planning and decision-making. Many service management processes and functions will link into this. Links to HR, facilities and other supporting services should also be established, maintained and utilized.

The challenge is transferring knowledge between parts of the organization. The knowledge needs to be in a form that is both applicable and easy to use.

If necessary, a gap analysis of knowledge transfer is undertaken. The output is a communications improvement plan, which recognizes that people receive and interpret knowledge in different ways, using different learning styles.

8.5.3 Managing data, information and knowledge

Knowledge rests on the management of the information and data that underpin it. To be efficient, this process needs to have an understanding of some key process inputs such as:

- What data is available
- The cost of capturing and maintaining data
- The value of that data
- How the data and information will be used
- Applicable policies, legislation, standards and other requirements
- Intellectual property and copyright issues.

Often data and information are collected with no clear understanding of how they will be used. Efficiency and effectiveness are delivered by establishing the requirements for information.

In order to make effective use of data in terms of delivering knowledge, it is essential to have a relevant architecture matched to the organization and the knowledge requirements.

Once the requirements have been defined and the architecture set up, data and information management requirements can be established to support knowledge management. For example:

- Information to be collected
- Maintenance of data
- Storage and retrieval
- Backup and recovery
- Publication and usage rights
- Security.

As with all ITIL processes and functions, the capture and use of data and information to support knowledge management needs regular review and attention for continual improvement.

Implementation of an SKMS helps reduce the costs of maintaining and managing services. It does this by increasing the efficiency of operational mechanisms while reducing the risks that may be caused by inaccurate or ineffective mechanisms. Useful materials may include:

- Training materials
- Business process documentation
- Process maps
- Known errors and workarounds
- Business and public calendars.

8.6 TRIGGERS, INPUTS, OUTPUTS AND INTERFACES (ST 4.7.6)

Knowledge management has many triggers, relating to every requirement for storing, maintaining or using knowledge, information or data within the organization.

Inputs to knowledge management include all knowledge, information and data used by the service provider, as well as relevant business data.

The key output of knowledge management is the knowledge required to make decisions and to manage the IT services; this is maintained within an SKMS.

Knowledge management has interfaces with every other service management process in every stage of the lifecycle. The SKMS can only be truly effective if all processes and activities use it to store and manage their information and data, so that the maximum value can be extracted.

8.7   INFORMATION MANAGEMENT (ST 4.7.7)

Creation of an SKMS can involve a large investment in tools to store and manage data, information and knowledge. Every organization will start this work in a different place and have its own vision of where it wants to be. For this reason there is no simple answer to the question, 'What tools and systems are needed to support knowledge management?'

In practice, an SKMS is likely to consist of a large number of tools and repositories, some running independently and others having links between them to allow cross-referencing and creation of added value.

8.8   CRITICAL SUCCESS FACTORS AND KEY PERFORMANCE INDICATORS (ST 4.7.8)

The efficiency and effectiveness of the process can be measured by identifying critical success factors (CSFs) for the process, each CSF being supported by key performance indicators (KPIs):

- **CSF** Availability of knowledge and information that helps to support management decision-making:
  - KPI Increased number of accesses to the SKMS by managers
  - KPI Increased percentage of SKMS searches by managers that receive a rating of 'good'
- **CSF** Reduced time and effort required to support and maintain services:
  - KPI Increased number of times that material is re-used in documentation such as procedures, test design and service desk scripts

- KPI Increased number of accesses to the SKMS by service operation teams
- KPI Reduced transfer of issues to other people and more resolution at lower staff levels.

8.9 CHALLENGES AND RISKS (ST 4.7.9)

Implementing knowledge management can be a difficult task. Most organizations already have stores of knowledge, information and data that meet many of their needs, and it can be challenging to justify the effort that would be needed to create a consistent architecture for managing these.

Each group or team within the service provider may own and manage the information that it uses, and may see knowledge management as interfering in its work. The challenge is to help all the stakeholders understand the added value that a more holistic approach to knowledge management can bring, and to continue to demonstrate this value as an SKMS is built.

The risks to knowledge management include:

- Focusing on the supporting tools, rather than on the creation of value
- Insufficient understanding of what knowledge, information and data are needed by the organization
- Lack of investment in the tools and people needed to support the SKMS
- Spending too much effort on knowledge capture while paying insufficient attention to knowledge transfer and re-use
- Storing and sharing knowledge and information that are not up to date and relevant
- Lack of support and commitment from stakeholders.

8.10   RELATIONSHIP WITH CONTINUAL SERVICE IMPROVEMENT (CSI 3.7)

Knowledge management plays a key role in continual service improvement. Each phase of the lifecycle captures data to gain knowledge and understanding, which in turn leads to wisdom. This is frequently referred to as the DIKW model (see Figure 8.1). Organizations often capture data but then fail to format and process it into information. They therefore cannot synthesize this information into knowledge or combine it with knowledge from others to generate wisdom. This applies to both services and processes; therefore knowledge management is pivotal for any improvement.

8.11   ROLES AND RESPONSIBILITIES (ST 6.4.11)

8.11.1 Knowledge management process owner

Responsibilities include:

- Carrying out the generic process owner role for the knowledge management process (see section 1.5)
- Creating the overall architecture for identification, capture and maintenance of knowledge within the organization.

8.11.2 Knowledge management process manager

Responsibilities include:

- Carrying out the generic process manager role for the knowledge management process (see section 1.5)
- Ensuring that all knowledge items can be accessed in an efficient and effective manner by those who need them

- Planning and managing support for knowledge management tools and processes
- Encouraging people throughout the service provider organization to contribute knowledge to the SKMS
- Acting as an adviser to business and IT personnel on knowledge management matters, including policy decisions on storage, value and worth.

8.11.3 Knowledge management process practitioner

Responsibilities include:

- Identifying, controlling and storing any information deemed to be pertinent to the services provided that is not available by other means
- Maintaining controlled knowledge items to ensure that they are current, relevant and valid
- Monitoring publicity regarding the knowledge information to ensure that information is not duplicated and is recognized as the central source.

The person carrying out this role is recognized as a central source of information and in some organizations is called a 'knowledge librarian'.

8.11.4 Knowledge creator

Creation and sharing of knowledge is often written into the job descriptions of people in many different roles within IT and the business.

9 Technology and implementation

9.1 GENERIC REQUIREMENTS FOR IT SERVICE MANAGEMENT TECHNOLOGY (SO 7.1)

The same technology should be used at all stages of the service lifecycle. Generally this includes:

- **Self-help** A web front end offering a menu-driven range of self-help and service requests. It should have a direct interface with the process-handling software at the back end
- **Workflow or process engine** To allow predefinition and control of defined processes such as incident lifecycle, request fulfilment lifecycle and change models. It should allow predefinition and management of responsibilities, activities, timescales, escalation paths and alerting
- **Integrated configuration management system (CMS)** To manage information about all the organization's IT infrastructure and other CIs, together with required attributes and relationships. It should support links, for example, to incidents, problems, known errors, change records and release records
- **Discovery, deployment and licensing technology** To populate or verify CMS data and assist in licence management. It can often also be used to deploy software, ideally with an interface to self-help
- **Remote control** To enable support personnel to take control of users' desktops to conduct investigations or correct settings. It must include appropriate security controls
- **Diagnostic utilities** Including scripts and case-based reasoning tools. Ideally it should present automated, context-sensitive scripts

- **Reporting** Tools should include good reporting capabilities and a means for providing data to industry-standard reporting packages and dashboards
- **Dashboards** To provide 'at a glance' visibility of overall IT service performance. Displays can also be included in management reports. Dynamic, customized web-based views can be very useful
- **Integration with business service management** To allow combined views of ITSM and business-related IT.

9.2   EVALUATION CRITERIA FOR TECHNOLOGY AND TOOLS (SD 7.2)

Some generic points that organizations should consider when selecting any service management tool include:

- Data handling, integration, import, export and conversion
- Data backup, control and security
- Ability to integrate multi-vendor components, existing and into the future
- Conformity with international open standards
- Usability, scalability and flexibility of implementation and usage
- Support options provided by the vendor, and credibility of the vendor and tool
- The platform the tool will run on and how this fits the IT strategy
- Training and other requirements for customizing, deploying and using the tool
- Costs: initial and ongoing.

It is generally best to select a fully integrated tool, but this must support the processes used by the organization, and extensive tool customization should be avoided.

Consideration should also be given to the organization's exact requirements. These should be documented in a statement of requirements. Tool requirements should be categorized using MoSCoW analysis:

- **M** – MUST have this
- **S** – SHOULD have this if at all possible
- **C** – COULD have this if it does not affect anything else
- **W** – WON'T have this, but WOULD like in the future.

Each proposed tool can be evaluated against these criteria to ensure that the most appropriate option is selected.

9.3   PRACTICES FOR PROCESS IMPLEMENTATION

9.3.1   Managing change in service operation (SO 8.1)

There are many things that could trigger a change in the service operation environment. These include changes to legislation, governance, and business needs, as well as new or upgraded infrastructure and applications.

Service operation staff must be involved in assessment of all changes, not just as members of the change advisory board (CAB) but at a sufficiently early stage that they can influence design decisions.

The measure of success for any change made to service operation is that customers do not experience any variation or outage. The effects should be invisible, apart from enhanced functionality, quality or financial savings resulting from the change.

9.3.2   Service operation and project management (SO 8.2)

It is important that all projects make use of project management processes. Many organizations treat service operation as 'business as usual' and do not use project management for activities such as major infrastructure upgrades or deployment of new or changed procedures.

Using project management processes can bring the following benefits:

- Project benefits are agreed and documented
- It is easier to see what is being done and how it is being managed
- Funding can be easier to obtain
- There is greater consistency and improved quality
- Objectives are more likely to be achieved, leading to higher credibility for operational groups.

9.3.3   Assessing and managing risk in service operation (SO 8.3)

Risk assessment and management is required throughout the service lifecycle. There are occasions, such as the following, when assessment of risk to service operation must be carried out and acted on very quickly:

- Risks from potential changes or known errors
- Failures or potential failures: these may be identified by event management, incident management or problem management, but also by warnings from manufacturers, suppliers or contractors
- Environmental risks: risks to the physical environment as well as political, commercial or industrial relations risks, which could lead to invoking IT service continuity

- Suppliers, particularly if they control key service components
- Security risks
- Support of new customers or services.

9.3.4 Operational staff in service design and transition (SO 8.4)

Activities during service design and service transition should involve staff from all IT groups to ensure that new components and services are designed, tested and implemented in a way that will provide the service utility and service warranty required.

Service operation staff must be involved during the early stages of design and transition to ensure that new services are fit for purpose from an operational perspective and supportable in the future. This will mean that:

- Services are capable of being supported from a technical and operational viewpoint with existing (or agreed additional) resources and skills
- There is no adverse impact on other practices, processes or schedules
- There are no unexpected operational costs
- There are no unexpected contractual or legal complications
- There are no complex support paths with multiple support departments or third parties.

Planning changes, and implementing them, does not involve technology alone. Thought must be given to awareness, cultural change, motivation and many other issues.

9.4 CHALLENGES, CRITICAL SUCCESS FACTORS AND RISKS RELATING TO IMPLEMENTING PRACTICES AND PROCESSES

9.4.1 Challenges (ST 9.1)

Challenges for service transition include:

- Enabling almost every business process and service in IT, resulting in a large customer and stakeholder group that is involved and impacted by service transition
- Managing many contacts, interfaces and relationships through service transition, including a variety of different customers, users, programmes, projects, suppliers and partners. Establishing 'Who is doing what, when and where?' and 'Who should be doing what, when and where?'
- Little harmonization and integration of the processes and disciplines that impact service transition, such as finance, engineering and human resource management
- Inherent differences among the legacy systems, new technology and human elements that result in unknown dependencies and are risky to change
- Achieving a balance between maintaining a stable live environment and being responsive to the business needs for changing the services
- Achieving a balance between pragmatism and bureaucracy
- Understanding the different stakeholder perspectives that underpin effective risk management within an organization.

9.4.2 Critical success factors (ST 9.2)

CSFs for service transition include:

- Understanding and managing the different stakeholder perspectives that underpin effective risk management within an organization, and establishing and maintaining stakeholder buy-in and commitment
- Having clearly defined relationships and interfaces with programme and project management
- Integrating with the other service lifecycle stages, processes and disciplines that impact service transition
- Automating processes to eliminate errors and reduce the cycle time
- Creating and maintaining new and updated knowledge in a form that people can find and use
- Being able to understand the service and technical configurations and their dependencies
- Demonstrating improved cycle time to deliver change with fewer variations in time, cost and quality predictions during and after transition
- Demonstrating that the benefits of establishing and improving the service transition practice and processes outweigh the costs (across the organization and services).

9.4.3 Risks (ST 9.3)

Implementing the service transition practice should not be made without recognizing the potential risk to services currently in transition and those releases that are planned. A baseline assessment of current service transitions and planned projects will help service transition to identify implementation risks. These risks include:

- Change in accountabilities, responsibilities and practices of existing projects that demotivate the workforce
- Alienation of some key support and operations staff
- Additional unplanned costs to services in transition
- Resistance to change and circumvention of the processes due to perceived bureaucracy.

Other implementation risks include:

- Excessive costs to the business generated by overly risk-averse service transition practices and plans
- Knowledge sharing (the wrong people may have access to information)
- Lack of maturity and integration of systems and tools, resulting in people 'blaming' technology for other shortcomings
- Poor integration between the processes, causing process isolation and a silo approach to delivering ITSM
- Loss of productive hours, higher costs, loss of revenue or perhaps even business failure as a result of poor service transition processes.

9.5　PLANNING AND IMPLEMENTING SERVICE MANAGEMENT TECHNOLOGIES (SO 8.5)

There are a number of factors to consider when deploying and implementing ITSM support tools:

- **Licences** The cost of service management tools is usually determined by the type and number of user licences needed. Most tools are modular, so the specific selection of modules also affects the price. It is important to plan the provision of licences to avoid unexpected costs. There are a number of different licence types:

- – Dedicated licences For staff who need frequent and prolonged use of the module (e.g. service desk staff)
- – Shared licences For staff who use the module regularly, but with significant times when it is not needed. The ratio of licences to users should be calculated to give sufficient use at acceptable cost
- – Web licences For staff who need occasional access, or remote access, or who only need limited functionality
- – Service on demand The charge is based on the number of hours the service is used. This is suitable for smaller organizations or very specialized tools that are not used often. It can also include tools licensed as part of a consulting exercise (e.g. for carrying out capacity modelling)

■ **Deployment** Many tools, especially discovery and event-monitoring tools, require deployment of clients or agents. This requires careful scheduling, planning and execution and should be subject to formal release and deployment management. Devices may need to be rebooted and this needs to be planned. Change management is used and the CMS updated. Particular care should be taken when planning deployment to laptops and other portable equipment that may not be connected all the time

■ **Capacity checks** It may be necessary to check for sufficient system resources (e.g. disk space, CPU, memory) when planning a deployment. Allow sufficient lead time for upgrading or replacing equipment, and check network capacity

■ **Timing of technology deployment** If tools are deployed too early, they can be seen as 'the solution' on their own and essential process improvements will not be carried out. If tools are deployed too late, it can be hard to implement the new process. People need to be trained in use of the tool as well as the new or updated process, and timing for this must be planned, possibly with additional training after the tools have gone live

■ **Type of introduction** The new tool often replaces an existing tool, and careful planning is needed for the transition. A phased approach can be more appropriate than a 'big bang' approach, but this depends on the exact circumstances. The key factor is planning what data needs to be migrated, and how. If data is being migrated, a data quality audit should be performed. An alternative approach is parallel running, in which case the old tool should run in a 'read only' mode to prevent mistakes.

9.6   TECHNOLOGY FOR IMPLEMENTING COLLABORATION, CONFIGURATION MANAGEMENT AND KNOWLEDGE MANAGEMENT

9.6.1   Collaboration (ST 7.2)

Collaboration is sharing tacit knowledge and working together to achieve goals. Typical tools to support this include:

■ Shared calendars and tasks
■ Threaded discussions
■ Email and instant messaging
■ Whiteboarding, videoconferencing and teleconferencing.

Communities are a good method for allowing groups spread across countries and time zones to collaborate. The community elects a leader to run the community and subject matter experts to contribute and evaluate knowledge. Tools to support online communities include:

- Community portals
- Email alias management
- Focus groups
- Repository for intellectual property, best practices and work examples
- Online events and net shows.

Recognition for contributions to the community encourages people to share.

Workflow management provides support for managing knowledge through a predefined workflow. This is often used in managing incidents, changes etc. Tools to support this typically provide:

- Workflow design
- Routeing objects and event services
- Gatekeeping at authorization checkpoints and state transition services.

9.6.2   Configuration management system (ST 7.3)

The CMS contains details about the attributes and history of each CI, and details of the important relationships between CIs. Ideally it should be linked to the definitive media library (DML); if this is not possible, then consider automating the comparison of CMS and DML.

The CMS should prevent unauthorized changes to the infrastructure or services. All changes should be recorded, and the status of CIs should be updated automatically if possible. Features that a CMS should provide include:

- Appropriate security controls, only allowing access that is required

- Support for complex CIs with hierarchic and networked relationships and automatic update of version when a component version changes
- Easy addition, modification and deletion of CIs, with automatic validation of input data, automatic detection of relationships where possible, and maintenance of history of all CIs
- Support for model numbers, version numbers and copy numbers
- Support for baselines
- Automatic identification of related CIs when managing incidents, problems and changes
- Good interrogation and reporting, including trend analysis and graphical representation of relationships.

Several tools may need to be integrated to provide a full solution. The CMS may be combined with the service management system, but integration may be done at the procedural or data level if this is more appropriate. Automated discovery tools can improve the efficiency and effectiveness of the CMS.

Ideally, a single tool should manage software assets from the start of systems analysis, but if this is not possible there must be a way to transfer information from development to the live CMS.

9.6.3   Knowledge management tools (ST 7.1)

Knowledge management tools support the maintenance of electronic documents and records. A record is evidence of an activity – such as minutes of a meeting – or details of an incident, problem or change. A document is evidence of intentions, and can include policy statements, plans and service level agreements (SLAs).

Knowledge management activities include:

- **Document management** To store, protect, archive, classify and retire documents and information
- **Records management** To store, protect, archive, classify and retire records
- **Content management** To store, maintain and retrieve documents and information on a system or website. Content management makes use of:
  - Web publishing tools, including conferencing, wikis and blogs
  - Word processing, flowcharting and presentation tools
  - Data and financial analysis
  - Publication and distribution
  - Content management systems (codifying, organizing, version control, document architectures).

9.7 THE DEMING CYCLE (CSI 3.7, 3.8, 5.5)

Planning and implementing service management technologies is not a project that ends; it is part of the process for supporting and improving the overall service management system.

The Deming Cycle, shown in Figure 9.1, is a four-stage cycle for quality improvement. The cycle is based on a process-led approach to management, with defined processes, measurement of activities and audited outputs.

The four stages of the Plan-Do-Check-Act cycle are:

- **Plan** Document the scope, goals and objectives; identify the processes, tools or whatever else is to be developed and deployed; define measurement systems; establish timelines and resources

Figure 9.1 Plan-Do-Check-Act cycle (Deming Cycle)

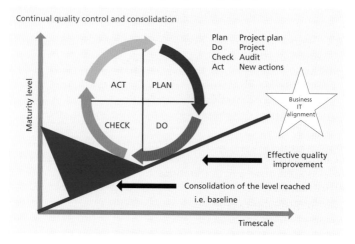

- **Do** Obtain the funding; carry out detailed design work; document the processes, roles and responsibilities; carry out training and communication; deploy the new process or tool. The Do stage also includes ongoing running of the new process or tool
- **Check** Monitor, measure and review, to ensure that the goals and objectives are being met. This includes reporting against plans, and conducting process assessments and audits. The key output of this stage should be identification of opportunities for improvement
- **Act** This stage is where improvements are actually implemented. It could include updating policies, processes, procedures, roles and responsibilities, tools or documents.

10 Qualifications

10.1 OVERVIEW

The ITIL qualification scheme has four levels:

- Foundation level
- Intermediate level (Lifecycle and Capability streams)
- ITIL Expert
- ITIL Master.

There are also further complementary service management qualifications available that can contribute (accumulating credits) towards achievement of the ITIL Expert. Further details of these can be found at:

www.itil-officialsite.com/Qualifications/
ComplementaryQualifications.aspx

10.2 FOUNDATION LEVEL

The Foundation level ensures candidates gain knowledge of the ITIL terminology, structure and basic concepts, and comprehend the core principles of ITIL practices for service management. Foundation represents two credits towards the ITIL Expert.

10.3 INTERMEDIATE LEVEL

There are two streams in the Intermediate level, assessing an individual's ability to analyse and apply concepts of ITIL:

- Lifecycle stream
- Capability stream.

10.3.1 Lifecycle stream

The Lifecycle stream is built around the five core publications and is for candidates wanting to gain knowledge within the service lifecycle context. Each module achieves three credits.

10.3.2 Capability stream

The Capability stream is built around four practitioner-based clusters and is for candidates wanting to gain knowledge of specific processes and roles. Each module achieves four credits:

- **Planning, protection and optimization (PPO)** Including capacity management, availability management, IT service continuity management, information security management, and demand management
- **Service offerings and agreements (SOA)** Including service portfolio management, service level management, service catalogue management, demand management, supplier management, and financial management for IT services
- **Release, control and validation (RCV)** Including change management, release and deployment management, service validation and testing, service asset and configuration management, knowledge management, request fulfilment, and change evaluation
- **Operational support and analysis (OSA)** Including event management, incident management, request fulfilment, problem management, access management, service desk, technical management, IT operations management and application management.

Candidates may take units from either of the streams to accumulate credits.

To complete the Intermediate level, the Managing Across the Lifecycle course (five credits) is required to bring together the full essence of a lifecycle approach to service management, consolidating knowledge gained across the qualification scheme.

10.4   ITIL EXPERT

Candidates automatically qualify for an ITIL Expert certificate once they have achieved the prerequisite 22 credits from Foundation (the mandatory initial unit) and Intermediate units (including Managing Across the Lifecycle, the mandatory final unit). No further examinations or courses are required.

10.5   ITIL MASTER

The ITIL Master qualification validates the capability of the candidate to apply the principles, methods and techniques of ITIL in the workplace.

To achieve the ITIL Master qualification, the candidate must be able to explain and justify how they selected and individually applied a range of knowledge, principles, methods and techniques from ITIL and supporting management techniques, to achieve desired business outcomes in one or more practical assignments.

To be eligible for the ITIL Master qualification, candidates must have reached the ITIL Expert level and worked in IT service management for at least five years in leadership, managerial or higher-management advisory levels.

11 Related guidance (ST Appendix C)

This chapter summarizes the frameworks, best practices, standards, models and quality systems that complement ITIL practices.

11.1 ITIL GUIDANCE AND WEB SERVICES

ITIL is part of the Best Management Practice portfolio, published by TSO. Further information can be found at:

www.best-management-practice.com

and on the official ITIL site at: www.itil-officialsite.com

The ITIL glossary is accessed via the official ITIL site.

11.2 QUALITY MANAGEMENT SYSTEM

It is helpful to align service management processes with any quality management system already present in an organization. Total Quality Management (TQM) and ISO 9000:2005 are widely used, as is the Plan-Do-Check-Act (PDCA) cycle, often referred to as the Deming Cycle.

More information can be found at www.iso.org and www.deming.org

11.3 RISK MANAGEMENT

Every organization should implement some form of risk management, appropriate to its size and needs. Risk is usually defined as 'uncertainty of outcome', and can have both positive and negative effects. *Management of Risk* (M_o_R®), ISO 31000,

Risk IT and ISO/IEC 27001 all provide guidance related to risk management. See Appendix G in *ITIL Service Operation* (Cabinet Office, 2011) for further description of risk management.

11.4   GOVERNANCE OF IT

Governance defines the rules, policies and processes an organization needs to follow, and makes sure they are implemented consistently.

There are two ISO standards that relate to governance. ISO 9004 provides board and executive level guidance, and ISO/IEC 38500 provides for corporate governance.

11.5   COBIT

Control OBjectives for Information and related Technology (COBIT) is a governance and control framework for IT management. COBIT looks at what needs to be achieved, and ITIL provides complementary guidance about how to achieve it.

Further information can be found at www.isaca.org and www.itgi.org

11.6   ISO/IEC 20000 SERVICE MANAGEMENT SERIES

ISO/IEC 20000 is the standard for ITSM, applying to both internal and external service providers, although the standard is currently to be extended with the development of Parts 3 and 4:

■ ISO/IEC 20000-1:2011 Part 1: Service management system requirements
■ ISO/IEC 20000-2:2012 Part 2: Guidance on the application of service management systems

- ISO/IEC 20000-3:2012 Part 3: Guidance on scope definition and applicability of ISO/IEC 20000-1
- ISO/IEC 20000-4:2007 Part 4: Process reference model
- ISO/IEC 20000-5:2010 Part 5: Exemplar implementation plan for ISO/IEC 20000-1
- BIP 0005: A manager's guide to service management
- BIP 0015: IT service management: self-assessment workbook (currently assesses against ITIL V2, to be revised via ITIL V3 complementary publications).

These documents provide a standard against which organizations can be assessed and certified with regard to the quality of their ITSM processes.

An ISO/IEC 20000 certification scheme was introduced in December 2005. A number of auditing organizations are accredited within the scheme to assess and certify organizations as compliant to the ISO/IEC 20000 standard and its content. The standard and ITIL are aligned, and ITIL best practices can help an organization looking to achieve ISO accreditation.

Further information can be found at www.iso.org or www.isoiec20000certification.com

11.7   ENVIRONMENTAL MANAGEMENT AND GREEN AND SUSTAINABLE IT

IT is a major user of energy, but can also support cultural and environmental changes as part of a green initiative. Green IT is about environmentally sustainable computing, from design through to disposal.

ISO 14001 is a series of standards related to an environment management system. Further details can be found at www.iso.org

11.8 ISO STANDARDS AND PUBLICATIONS FOR IT

There are many ISO standards and publications with relevance for IT and ITIL. Further details can be found at www.iso.org

Relevant examples include:

- ISO 9241: covers aspects that may affect the utility of a service
- ISO/IEC JTC1: deals with IT standards and publications
- The SC27 sub-committee develops ISO/IEC 27000, which relates to information security management
- The SC7 sub-committee develops other relevant standards including ISO/IEC 20000 (service management), ISO/IEC 15504 (process assessment or SPICE) and ISO/IEC 19770 (software asset management).

11.9 ITIL AND THE OSI FRAMEWORK

The Open Systems Interconnection (OSI) framework was developed by ISO at the same time as ITIL V1 was written. Common expressions such as installation, moves, additions and changes (IMAC) are OSI terminology, although IT practitioners may not realize this.

11.10 PROGRAMME AND PROJECT MANAGEMENT

Programme management can be used to deliver complex pieces of work, using interrelated projects. *Managing Successful Programmes* (MSP®) provides guidance related to programme management.

Portfolio, Programme and Project Offices (P3O®) provides guidance on managing these three areas together.

Project management guidance is found in PRojects IN Controlled Environments (PRINCE2®) and the Project Management Body of Knowledge (PMBOK).

Details of the above publications can be found at:

www.msp-officialsite.com

www.p3o-officialsite.com

www.prince-officialsite.com

www.pmi.org

11.11 ORGANIZATIONAL CHANGE

The organizational aspects of IT change need to be considered to ensure that changes are successful. Kotter's eight steps for organizational change (www.johnkotter.com) are referenced in *ITIL Service Transition* and *ITIL Continual Service Improvement* (Cabinet Office, 2011). See section on further guidance for details.

11.12 SKILLS FRAMEWORK FOR THE INFORMATION AGE

Skills Framework for the Information Age (SFIA) provides a common framework for IT skills. This supports job standardization, skills audits and skills planning exercises.

SFIA is a two-dimensional matrix showing areas of work and levels of responsibility. Further information can be found at www.sfia-online.org

11.13 CARNEGIE MELLON: CMMI AND eSCM FRAMEWORKS

The Capability Maturity Model Integration (CMMI) is a process improvement approach applicable to projects, divisions or entire organizations.

The eSourcing Capability Model for Service Providers (eSCM-SP) is a framework to improve the relationship between IT service providers and customers.

SCAMPI assessments can be carried out against CMMI–Standard CMMI Appraisal Method for Process Improvement. More information can be found at www.cmmiinstitute.com

11.14 BALANCED SCORECARD

The balanced scorecard approach to strategic management was developed by Drs Robert Kaplan and David Norton. It views an organization from four perspectives to balance out the financial perspective which drives many decisions. The perspectives are:

- Learning and growth
- Business process
- Customer
- Financial.

The scorecard can be applied to IT quality performance and service operation performance. More information can be found at www.scorecardsupport.com

11.15 SIX SIGMA

Six Sigma is a data-driven process improvement approach. It identifies defects that lead to improvement opportunities. Six Sigma tries to reduce process variation. It has two primary sub-methodologies:

■ DMAIC – define, measure, analyse, improve, control
■ DMADV – define, measure, analyse, design, verify.

Further information can be found online, including Six Sigma overviews and training.

Further guidance and contact points

TSO

PO Box 29
Norwich NR3 1GN
United Kingdom
Tel: +44(0) 870 600 5522
Fax: +44(0) 870 600 5533
Email: customer.services@tso.co.uk
www.tso.co.uk

*it*SMF UK

150 Wharfedale Road
Winnersh Triangle
Wokingham
Berkshire RG41 5RB
United Kingdom
Tel: +44(0) 118 918 6500
Fax: +44(0) 118 969 9749
Email: publications@itsmf.co.uk
www.itsmf.co.uk

BEST PRACTICE WITH ITIL

The ITIL publication portfolio consists of a unique library of titles that offer guidance on quality IT services and best practices. The ITIL 2011 lifecycle suite (five core publications) comprises:

Cabinet Office (2011). *ITIL Service Strategy*. The Stationery Office, London.

Cabinet Office (2011). *ITIL Service Design*. The Stationery Office, London.

Cabinet Office (2011). *ITIL Service Transition*. The Stationery Office, London.

Cabinet Office (2011). *ITIL Service Operation*. The Stationery Office, London.

Cabinet Office (2011). *ITIL Continual Service Improvement*. The Stationery Office, London.

ITIL-DERIVED GUIDANCE

There is a range of derived publications which support the core guidance. Details of all publications can be found in the publications library section of the Best Management Practice website: www.best-management-practice.com/Publications-Library/IT-Service-Management-ITIL

ABOUT *it*SMF

*it*SMF is the only truly independent and internationally recognized forum for IT service management professionals worldwide. Since 1991 this not-for-profit organization has been a prominent player in the ongoing development and promotion of IT service management best practice, standards and qualifications. Globally, *it*SMF now boasts more than 6,000 member companies, blue-chip and public-sector alike, covering in excess of 70,000 individuals spread over more than 50 international chapters.

Each chapter is a separate legal entity and is largely autonomous. *it*SMF International provides an overall steering and support function to existing and emerging chapters. It has its own website at www.itsmfi.org

The UK chapter has more than 8,000 members: it offers a flourishing annual conference, online bookstore, regular regional meetings, seminars and special interest groups and numerous other benefits for members. Its website is at www.itsmf.co.uk

ABOUT TSO

TSO is one of the largest publishers by volume in the UK, publishing more than 9,000 titles a year in print and digital formats for a wide range of clients.

TSO has a long history in publishing best-practice guidance related to project, programme and IT service management. Working with partners including *it*SMF, the Project Management Institute, Service Management 101 and APMG-International, we publish guidance for a global range of management disciplines.

For more information on our publications and to browse our resources, please visit www.internationalbestpractice.com

Glossary

A candidate is expected to understand the following terms after completing an RCV course.

These terms are as defined in the standard ITIL glossary. The core publication titles (*ITIL Service Strategy, ITIL Service Design, ITIL Service Operation, ITIL Service Transition* and *ITIL Continual Service Improvement)* included in parentheses at the beginning of the definition indicate where a reader can find more information.

acceptance
Formal agreement that an IT service, process, plan or other deliverable is complete, accurate, reliable and meets its specified requirements. Acceptance is usually preceded by change evaluation or testing and is often required before proceeding to the next stage of a project or process.

assembly
(*ITIL Service Transition*) A configuration item that is made up of a number of other CIs. For example, a server CI may contain CIs for CPUs, disks, memory etc.; an IT service CI may contain many hardware, software and other CIs. *See also* build; component CI.

asset
(*ITIL Service Strategy*) Any resource or capability. The assets of a service provider include anything that could contribute to the delivery of a service. Assets can be one of the following types: management, organization, process, knowledge, people, information, applications, infrastructure or financial capital.

asset register

(*ITIL Service Transition*) A list of fixed assets that includes their ownership and value. *See also* fixed asset management.

attribute

(*ITIL Service Transition*) A piece of information about a configuration item. Examples are name, location, version number and cost. Attributes of CIs are recorded in a configuration management database (CMDB) and maintained as part of a configuration management system (CMS). *See also* relationship.

audit

Formal inspection and verification to check whether a standard or set of guidelines is being followed, that records are accurate, or that efficiency and effectiveness targets are being met. An audit may be carried out by internal or external groups.

availability

(*ITIL Service Design*) Ability of an IT service or other configuration item to perform its agreed function when required. Availability is determined by reliability, maintainability, serviceability, performance and security. Availability is usually calculated as a percentage. This calculation is often based on agreed service time and downtime. It is best practice to calculate availability of an IT service using measurements of the business output.

back-out

(*ITIL Service Transition*) An activity that restores a service or other configuration item to a previous baseline. Back-out is used as a form of remediation when a change or release is not successful.

baseline

(*ITIL Continual Service Improvement*) (*ITIL Service Transition*) A snapshot that is used as a reference point. Many snapshots may be taken and recorded over time but only some will be used as baselines. For example:

- An ITSM baseline can be used as a starting point to measure the effect of a service improvement plan
- A performance baseline can be used to measure changes in performance over the lifetime of an IT service
- A configuration baseline can be used as part of a back-out plan to enable the IT infrastructure to be restored to a known configuration if a change or release fails.

budgeting

The activity of predicting and controlling the spending of money. Budgeting consists of a periodic negotiation cycle to set future budgets (usually annual) and the day-to-day monitoring and adjusting of current budgets.

build

(*ITIL Service Transition*) The activity of assembling a number of configuration items to create part of an IT service. The term is also used to refer to a release that is authorized for distribution – for example, server build or laptop build. *See also* configuration baseline.

build environment

(*ITIL Service Transition*) A controlled environment where applications, IT services and other builds are assembled prior to being moved into a test or live environment.

business objective

(*ITIL Service Strategy*) The objective of a business process, or of the business as a whole. Business objectives support the business vision, provide guidance for the IT strategy, and are often supported by IT services.

business relationship management

(*ITIL Service Strategy*) The process responsible for maintaining a positive relationship with customers. Business relationship management identifies customer needs and ensures that the service provider is able to meet these needs with an appropriate catalogue of services. This process has strong links with service level management.

capacity

(*ITIL Service Design*) The maximum throughput that a configuration item or IT service can deliver. For some types of CI, capacity may be the size or volume – for example, a disk drive.

change advisory board (CAB)

(*ITIL Service Transition*) A group of people that support the assessment, prioritization, authorization and scheduling of changes. A change advisory board is usually made up of representatives from: all areas within the IT service provider; the business; and third parties such as suppliers.

change schedule

(*ITIL Service Transition*) A document that lists all authorized changes and their planned implementation dates, as well as the estimated dates of longer-term changes. A change schedule is sometimes called a forward schedule of change, even though it also contains information about changes that have already been implemented.

change window

(*ITIL Service Transition*) A regular, agreed time when changes or releases may be implemented with minimal impact on services. Change windows are usually documented in service level agreements.

charter

(*ITIL Service Strategy*) A document that contains details of a new service, a significant change or other significant project. Charters are typically authorized by service portfolio management or by a project management office. The term charter is also used to describe the act of authorizing the work required to complete the service change or project. *See also* service charter.

CI type

(*ITIL Service Transition*) A category that is used to classify configuration items. The CI type identifies the required attributes and relationships for a configuration record. Common CI types include hardware, document, user etc.

component

A general term that is used to mean one part of something more complex. For example, a computer system may be a component of an IT service; an application may be a component of a release unit. Components that need to be managed should be configuration items.

component CI

(*ITIL Service Transition*) A configuration item that is part of an assembly. For example, a CPU or memory CI may be part of a server CI.

configuration

(*ITIL Service Transition*) A generic term used to describe a group of configuration items that work together to deliver an IT service, or a recognizable part of an IT service. Configuration is also used to describe the parameter settings for one or more configuration items.

configuration baseline

(*ITIL Service Transition*) The baseline of a configuration that has been formally agreed and is managed through the change management process. A configuration baseline is used as a basis for future builds, releases and changes.

configuration control

(*ITIL Service Transition*) The activity responsible for ensuring that adding, modifying or removing a configuration item is properly managed – for example, by submitting a request for change or service request.

configuration identification

(*ITIL Service Transition*) The activity responsible for collecting information about configuration items and their relationships, and loading this information into the configuration management database. Configuration identification is also responsible for labelling the configuration items themselves, so that the corresponding configuration records can be found.

configuration item (CI)

(*ITIL Service Transition*) Any component or other service asset that needs to be managed in order to deliver an IT service. Information about each configuration item is recorded in a configuration record within the configuration management system and is maintained throughout its lifecycle by service asset and configuration management. Configuration items are under the control of change management. They typically include IT services, hardware, software, buildings, people and formal documentation such as process documentation and service level agreements.

configuration management database (CMDB)

(*ITIL Service Transition*) A database used to store configuration records throughout their lifecycle. The configuration management system maintains one or more configuration management databases, and each database stores attributes of configuration items, and relationships with other configuration items.

configuration record

(*ITIL Service Transition*) A record containing the details of a configuration item. Each configuration record documents the lifecycle of a single configuration item. Configuration records are stored in a configuration management database and maintained as part of a configuration management system.

configuration structure

(*ITIL Service Transition*) The hierarchy and other relationships between all the configuration items that comprise a configuration.

continual service improvement (CSI)

(*ITIL Continual Service Improvement*) A stage in the lifecycle of a service. Continual service improvement ensures that services are aligned with changing business needs by identifying and implementing improvements to IT services that support business processes. The performance of the IT service provider is continually measured and improvements are made to processes, IT services and IT infrastructure in order to increase efficiency, effectiveness and cost effectiveness. Continual service improvement includes the seven-step improvement process. Although this process is associated with continual service improvement, most processes have activities that take place across multiple stages of the service lifecycle.

contract

A legally binding agreement between two or more parties.

course corrections

Changes made to a plan or activity that has already started to ensure that it will meet its objectives. Course corrections are made as a result of monitoring progress.

CSI register

(*ITIL Continual Service Improvement*) A database or structured document used to record and manage improvement opportunities throughout their lifecycle.

culture

A set of values that is shared by a group of people, including expectations about how people should behave, their ideas, beliefs and practices.

customer

Someone who buys goods or services. The customer of an IT service provider is the person or group who defines and agrees the service level targets. The term is also sometimes used informally to mean user – for example, 'This is a customer-focused organization.'

customer-facing service

(*ITIL Service Design*) An IT service that is visible to the customer. These are normally services that support the customer's business processes and facilitate one or more outcomes desired by the customer. All live customer-facing services, including those available for deployment, are recorded in the service catalogue along with customer-visible information about deliverables, prices, contact points, ordering and request processes. Other information such as relationships to supporting services and other CIs will also be recorded for internal use by the IT service provider.

definitive media library (DML)

(*ITIL Service Transition*) One or more locations in which the definitive and authorized versions of all software configuration items are securely stored. The definitive media library may also contain associated configuration items such as licences and documentation. It is a single logical storage area even if there are multiple locations. The definitive media library is controlled by service asset and configuration management and is recorded in the configuration management system.

deliverable

Something that must be provided to meet a commitment in a service level agreement or a contract. It is also used in a more informal way to mean a planned output of any process.

design coordination

(*ITIL Service Design*) The process responsible for coordinating all service design activities, processes and resources. Design coordination ensures the consistent and effective design of new or changed IT services, service management information systems, architectures, technology, processes, information and metrics.

effectiveness

(*ITIL Continual Service Improvement*) A measure of whether the objectives of a process, service or activity have been achieved. An effective process or activity is one that achieves its agreed objectives.

efficiency

(*ITIL Continual Service Improvement*) A measure of whether the right amount of resource has been used to deliver a process, service or activity. An efficient process achieves its objectives with the minimum amount of time, money, people or other resources.

emergency change

(*ITIL Service Transition*) A change that must be introduced as soon as possible – for example, to resolve a major incident or implement a security patch. The change management process will normally have a specific procedure for handling emergency changes. *See also* emergency change advisory board.

emergency change advisory board (ECAB)

(*ITIL Service Transition*) A subgroup of the change advisory board that makes decisions about emergency changes. Membership may be decided at the time a meeting is called, and depends on the nature of the emergency change.

environment

(*ITIL Service Transition*) A subset of the IT infrastructure that is used for a particular purpose – for example, live environment, test environment, build environment. Also used in the term 'physical environment' to mean the accommodation, air conditioning, power system etc. Environment is used as a generic term to mean the external conditions that influence or affect something.

fit for purpose

(*ITIL Service Strategy*) The ability to meet an agreed level of utility. Fit for purpose is also used informally to describe a process, configuration item, IT service etc. that is capable of meeting its objectives or service levels. Being fit for purpose requires suitable design, implementation, control and maintenance.

fit for use

(*ITIL Service Strategy*) The ability to meet an agreed level of warranty. Being fit for use requires suitable design, implementation, control and maintenance.

fixed asset

(*ITIL Service Transition*) A tangible business asset that has a long-term useful life (for example, a building, a piece of land, a server or a software licence). *See also* configuration item.

fixed asset management

(*ITIL Service Transition*) The process responsible for tracking and reporting the value and ownership of fixed assets throughout their lifecycle. Fixed asset management maintains the asset register and is usually carried out by the overall business, rather than by the IT organization. Fixed asset management is sometimes called financial asset management and is not described in detail within the core ITIL publications.

impact

(*ITIL Service Operation*) (*ITIL Service Transition*) A measure of the effect of an incident, problem or change on business processes. Impact is often based on how service levels will be affected. Impact and urgency are used to assign priority.

information security management (ISM)

(*ITIL Service Design*) The process responsible for ensuring that the confidentiality, integrity and availability of an organization's assets, information, data and IT services match the agreed needs of the business. Information security management supports business security and has a wider scope than that of the IT service provider, and includes handling of paper, building access, phone calls etc. for the entire organization.

knowledge base

(*ITIL Service Transition*) A logical database containing data and information used by the service knowledge management system.

known error

(*ITIL Service Operation*) A problem that has a documented root cause and a workaround. Known errors are created and managed throughout their lifecycle by problem management. Known errors may also be identified by development or suppliers.

known error database (KEDB)

(*ITIL Service Operation*) A database containing all known error records. This database is created by problem management and used by incident and problem management. The known error database may be part of the configuration management system, or may be stored elsewhere in the service knowledge management system.

live environment

(*ITIL Service Transition*) A controlled environment containing live configuration items used to deliver IT services to customers.

normal change

(*ITIL Service Transition*) A change that is not an emergency change or a standard change. Normal changes follow the defined steps of the change management process.

operational level agreement (OLA)

(*ITIL Continual Service Improvement*) (*ITIL Service Design*) An agreement between an IT service provider and another part of the same organization. It supports the IT service provider's delivery of IT services to customers and defines the goods or services to be provided and the responsibilities of both parties. For example, there could be an operational level agreement:

- Between the IT service provider and a procurement department to obtain hardware in agreed times
- Between the service desk and a support group to provide incident resolution in agreed times.

See also service level agreement.

outcome

The result of carrying out an activity, following a process, or delivering an IT service etc. The term is used to refer to intended results as well as to actual results.

post-implementation review (PIR)

A review that takes place after a change or a project has been implemented. It determines if the change or project was successful, and identifies opportunities for improvement.

priority

(*ITIL Service Operation*) (*ITIL Service Transition*) A category used to identify the relative importance of an incident, problem or change. Priority is based on impact and urgency, and is used to identify required times for actions to be taken. For example, the service level agreement may state that Priority 2 incidents must be resolved within 12 hours.

programme

A number of projects and activities that are planned and managed together to achieve an overall set of related objectives and other outcomes.

project

A temporary organization, with people and other assets, that is required to achieve an objective or other outcome. Each project has a lifecycle that typically includes initiation, planning, execution, and closure. Projects are usually managed using a formal methodology such as PRojects IN Controlled Environments (PRINCE2) or the Project Management Body of Knowledge (PMBOK). *See also* charter.

projected service outage (PSO)

(*ITIL Service Transition*) A document that identifies the effect of planned changes, maintenance activities and test plans on agreed service levels.

quality

The ability of a product, service or process to provide the intended value. For example, a hardware component can be considered to be of high quality if it performs as expected and delivers the required reliability. Process quality also requires an ability to monitor effectiveness and efficiency, and to improve them if necessary.

relationship

A connection or interaction between two people or things. In business relationship management, it is the interaction between the IT service provider and the business. In service asset and configuration management, it is a link between two configuration items that identifies a dependency or connection between them. For example, applications may be linked to the servers they run on, and IT services have many links to all the configuration items that contribute to that IT service.

release

(*ITIL Service Transition*) One or more changes to an IT service that are built, tested and deployed together. A single release may include changes to hardware, software, documentation, processes and other components.

release identification

(*ITIL Service Transition*) A naming convention used to uniquely identify a release. The release identification typically includes a reference to the configuration item and a version number – for example, Microsoft Office 2010 SR2.

release package

(*ITIL Service Transition*) A set of configuration items that will be built, tested and deployed together as a single release. Each release package will usually include one or more release units.

release record

(*ITIL Service Transition*) A record that defines the content of a release. A release record has relationships with all configuration items that are affected by the release. Release records may be in the configuration management system or elsewhere in the service knowledge management system.

release unit

(*ITIL Service Transition*) Components of an IT service that are normally released together. A release unit typically includes sufficient components to perform a useful function. For example, one release unit could be a desktop PC, including hardware, software, licences, documentation etc. A different release unit may be the complete payroll application, including IT operations procedures and user training.

requirement

(*ITIL Service Design*) A formal statement of what is needed – for example, a service level requirement, a project requirement or the required deliverables for a process.

service acceptance criteria (SAC)

(*ITIL Service Transition*) A set of criteria used to ensure that an IT service meets its functionality and quality requirements and that the IT service provider is ready to operate the new IT service when it has been deployed.

service catalogue

(*ITIL Service Design*) (*ITIL Service Strategy*) A database or structured document with information about all live IT services, including those available for deployment. The service catalogue is part of the service portfolio and contains information about two types of IT service: customer-facing services that are visible to the business; and supporting services required by the service provider to deliver customer-facing services.

service charter

(*ITIL Service Design*) (*ITIL Service Strategy*) A document that contains details of a new or changed service. New service introductions and significant service changes are documented in a charter and authorized by service portfolio management. Service charters are passed to the service design lifecycle stage where a new or modified service design package will be created. The term charter is also used to describe the act of authorizing the work required by each stage of the service lifecycle with respect to the new or changed service. *See also* service portfolio; service catalogue.

service design package (SDP)

(*ITIL Service Design*) Document(s) defining all aspects of an IT service and its requirements through each stage of its lifecycle. A service design package is produced for each new IT service, major change or IT service retirement.

service level agreement (SLA)

(*ITIL Continual Service Improvement*) (*ITIL Service Design*) An agreement between an IT service provider and a customer. A service level agreement describes the IT service, documents service level targets, and specifies the responsibilities of the IT service provider and the customer. A single agreement may cover multiple IT services or multiple customers. *See also* operational level agreement.

service level target

(*ITIL Continual Service Improvement*) (*ITIL Service Design*) A commitment that is documented in a service level agreement. Service level targets are based on service level requirements, and are needed to ensure that the IT service is able to meet business objectives. They should be SMART, and are usually based on key performance indicators.

service model

(*ITIL Service Strategy*) A model that shows how service assets interact with customer assets to create value. Service models describe the structure of a service (how the configuration items fit together) and the dynamics of the service (activities, flow of resources and interactions). A service model can be used as a template or blueprint for multiple services.

service portfolio

(*ITIL Service Strategy*) The complete set of services that is managed by a service provider. The service portfolio is used to manage the entire lifecycle of all services, and includes three categories: service pipeline (proposed or in development), service catalogue (live or available for deployment), and retired services.

service request

(*ITIL Service Operation*) A formal request from a user for something to be provided – for example, a request for information or advice; to reset a password; or to install a workstation for a new user. Service requests are managed by the request fulfilment process, usually in conjunction with the service desk. Service requests may be linked to a request for change as part of fulfilling the request.

specification

A formal definition of requirements. A specification may be used to define technical or operational requirements, and may be internal or external. Many public standards consist of a code of practice and a specification. The specification defines the standard against which an organization can be audited.

stakeholder

A person who has an interest in an organization, project, IT service etc. Stakeholders may be interested in the activities, targets, resources or deliverables. Stakeholders may include customers, partners, employees, shareholders, owners etc.

status accounting

(*ITIL Service Transition*) The activity responsible for recording and reporting the lifecycle of each configuration item.

supplier

(*ITIL Service Design*) (*ITIL Service Strategy*) A third party responsible for supplying goods or services that are required to deliver IT services. Examples of suppliers include commodity hardware and software vendors, network and telecom providers, and outsourcing organizations.

test

(*ITIL Service Transition*) An activity that verifies that a configuration item, IT service, process etc. meets its specification or agreed requirements. *See also* acceptance.

transition

(*ITIL Service Transition*) A change in state, corresponding to a movement of an IT service or other configuration item from one lifecycle status to the next.

transition planning and support

(*ITIL Service Transition*) The process responsible for planning all service transition processes and coordinating the resources that they require.

urgency

(*ITIL Service Design*) (*ITIL Service Transition*) A measure of how long it will be until an incident, problem or change has a significant impact on the business. For example, a high-impact incident may have low urgency if the impact will not affect the business until the end of the financial year. Impact and urgency are used to assign priority.

utility

(*ITIL Service Strategy*) The functionality offered by a product or service to meet a particular need. Utility can be summarized as 'what the service does', and can be used to determine whether a service is able to meet its required outcomes, or is 'fit for purpose'. The business value of an IT service is created by the combination of utility and warranty.

validation

(*ITIL Service Transition*) An activity that ensures a new or changed IT service, process, plan or other deliverable meets the needs of the business. Validation ensures that business requirements are met even though these may have changed since the original design. *See also* acceptance.

verification

(*ITIL Service Transition*) An activity that ensures that a new or changed IT service, process, plan or other deliverable is complete, accurate, reliable and matches its design specification. *See also* acceptance; validation.

verification and audit

(*ITIL Service Transition*) The activities responsible for ensuring that information in the configuration management system is accurate and that all configuration items have been identified and recorded. Verification includes routine checks that are part of other processes – for example, verifying the serial number of a desktop PC when a user logs an incident. Audit is a periodic, formal check.

version

(*ITIL Service Transition*) A version is used to identify a specific baseline of a configuration item. Versions typically use a naming convention that enables the sequence or date of each baseline to be identified. For example, payroll application version 3 contains updated functionality from version 2.

warranty

(*ITIL Service Strategy*) Assurance that a product or service will meet agreed requirements. This may be a formal agreement such as a service level agreement or contract, or it may be a marketing message or brand image. Warranty refers to the ability of a service to be available when needed, to provide the required capacity, and to provide the required reliability in terms of continuity and security. Warranty can be summarized as 'how the service is delivered', and can be used to determine whether a service is 'fit for use'. The business value of an IT service is created by the combination of utility and warranty.